Table of Contents

Betty Boyink presented President Ford with a quilt she made using her patterns on July 17, 1975, at the White House in the Oval Office. *(Official White House Photograph)*

A Word About Betty . . .

Highlighting Betty's career as a quilter was presenting a Bicentennial Quilt to President Ford in the Oval Office of the White House in July, 1975. She is also honored to have an evening skirt as part of the Smithsonian Institute's collection of Bicentennial memorabilia.

Betty marketed Official ARBA Bicentennial Quilt & Pillow Patterns of her design during this time.

A National Quilting Association Certified Teacher, Betty teaches and lectures in addition to being a professional seamstress. She is on the Advisory Board of the Sewing Department of Ottawa Vocational School.

She has directed several quilt shows/seminars including the West Michigan Quilting Seminar.

BETTY BOYINK • 818 Sheldon Road, Grand Haven, Michigan 49417

Soft Sculpture Baskets

In just a few easy steps, you can have a fabric, soft sculpture basket for any season of the year: Easter baskets for children, summer baskets as fruit containers, fall baskets as table decorations, or winter holiday baskets to hold greeting cards.

Plant holder baskets add flair to the special plant; a baby's supplies basket within easy reach is a must; quilter's or stitcher's basket filled with supplies should be kept handy at all times; a graduation, shower, or wedding gift basket is ideal for that someone special; and the list could go on and on.

Baskets are fun to make! Instructions presented here are relatively easy and can be adapted to your own creative design. Creative adaptations you might like to do include a Christmas tree ornament, a basket table favor, or a vanity basket to hold rings, jewelry and trinkets. Also, the next time you give someone a gift, consider making a basket home for that gift to make it extra special.

In using baskets for plants, a separate container (perhaps the bottom half of a plastic milk carton or two-pound margarine container) should be inserted to keep moisture away from the fabric basket. Baskets used for baby supplies and other soiling commodities should also be protected with a plastic liner or baggie. If you make baskets for these purposes, acquire the container first and make the basket to fit the protective liner.

Part of the charm of fabric baskets is that "little is cute." Quilting class students that have made large baskets have reported some of the charm had been lost in the larger size. Also, you will find baskets hold up better without being too tall or too big around. Soft baskets are pictured, but if you prefer more firmness, simply add interfacing (buckrum would be even stiffer). Cardboard is not recommended.

Being completely fabric and all prewashed supplies, soft sculpture baskets are easily freshened up by just washing. Easter baskets with chocolate stain may be washed with very hot water and liquid detergent right on the spot. If a brown stain remains, sponge with hydrogen peroxide. Fruit basket stains may be handled in a similar manner.

Materials Required:
½-yard or bits and pieces of coordinating prewashed fabric for basket sides and bottom.
⅓-yard coordinated fabric for lining
¼-yard of very firm bonded batting (or layers of lighter weight batting)
⅓-yard muslin inner lining or support fabric
Assorted laces, ribbons and trims — 24 inches to go around basket or 15 to 20 inches for basket handle

First step is to determine what the sides of your basket will be. By far, the easiest is one piece of fabric for the sides. An applique section with fill-in around string or a string basket are also easy to do. Pieced log cabin or pieced basket weave (patterns on pages 7-11) would take a little more time.

Basket size is as important a part of the first step as determining the design of the side. Material requirements presented here are given for a standard basket 6 inches high by 24 inches circumference. If you require a larger or smaller basket, lengthen or shorten the 6-inch and/or 24-inch dimensions. For example . . . a quart of strawberries fits in a 4½-inch high by 18-inch basket, a 4-inch potted plant requires a 4-inch high by 17-inch basket, and Christmas tree ornaments ideal size is 2 inches by 7½ inches. Christmas tree ornament size could also be used as table favors or napkin holders.

If you want a head start on the sides of your basket, you might even choose one of the pre-quilted fabrics and skip over to the basket construction instructions. However, if you do use "cheater's fabric" (a fun term quilters have adopted for pre-quilted fabric), please challenge yourself with a design or pattern illustrated in this book for your next basket.

A good average size side for a basket is 6 inches high by 24 inches around. Next step is to piece, applique, quilt or cut a section of fabric this dimension plus seam allowances.

If it is a **single fabric side,** cut your fabric 7 inches by 25 inches. Batting, muslin or backing fabric should be cut 1 inch larger all the way around. As you quilt back and forth, this excess batting and backing will be "gathered in" a little. It is easier to have some excess to trim off, rather than run short.

Now, either machine or hand quilt a design. One suggestion would be to use a wide zig-zag quilting up and down the basket. Up and down quilting provides greater support to have the basket sit upright; whereas circumferential quilting leads to drooping. You will need enough quilting to hold layers together nicely.

You also might consider adding a **fabric three-dimensional flower** or flowers to a plain basket or even one of the string baskets described below. Fabric petals pattern is on page 7.

Cut two of the flower shapes for each petal desired from a flower color fabric that coordinates with your basket. Also cut out the batting this shape. With right sides together and the batting on the underneath side (so it does not get caught in the presser foot of your sewing machine), sew around the edge of the petal . . . leaving an opening at the base for turning.

A leaf or outer petal effect can be achieved by using the larger petal or leaf pattern. Petals and leaves may be pointed or rounded.

Lay the six petals of the flower on the leaf petals and sew around the center. All raw edges can be concealed with a circle of fabric sewn in place over them. Baste near the edge of the circle and draw up a little to aid in turning under the edges of this circle. Hand sew in place . . . tucking in a little extra stuffing when you are more than half way. Next, hand sew your flower in place on the finished basket.

If you have made a single flower or double flower without leaves behind it, add individual leaves. This is the same template and assembly method used on the quilted bell pull flower and leaf pictured on the cover.

For the **string pieced side** (also shown on the cover), start with a 7-inch by 25-inch strip of muslin, a piece of batting a little larger, and a piece of backing muslin fabric the same size as the batting.

Strings should be cut 25 inches in length, but may vary in width from ½ to 2 inches, or may all be the same width. Starting at the bottom of the basket, lay the first string right side up . . . matching bottom edges . . . pin baste, and stitch ¼-inch from bottom edge. With right sides together, lay down the next string over the first string and sew ¼-inch seam allowance at top edge of fabric. Fold up the newly sewn string toward the top. Sew one, two or three more strings in the same manner.

Always start sewing each new strip from the same edge to prevent puckering. Also, hold tightly as the fabric feeds through your sewing machine to prevent further puckering . . . since the batting might want to creep differently than the two layers of fabric.

You are sewing through the fabric, batting, and backing all at the same time. In this way, you are quilting as-you-go, even though you will not see any quilting on the outside when it is finished. Add braids, lace trim or ribbon for a decorative effect.

For the **string going up and down** it is basically the same construction for the basket side as when you have the strings going around the basket. Start with a piece of muslin backing and batting 8 inches x 27 inches. Sew a fabric string on the edge. With right sides together, lay a second string on top of the first and sew a ¼-inch seam allowance. Fold open towards the other end and continue sewing strings in this manner until the whole basket side is covered.

You will need to always sew from top to bottom to prevent puckering. Since you have quilted the basket while sewing it together, you are ready to proceed with the construction steps.

If you have decided to **applique something on the basket** side, you may either choose to design a 6-inch by 24-inch pattern to fit the entire circumference or just a portion on one side of the basket.

The sunbonnet and tulip patterns are on page 8, but you may substitute the applique design of your choice. Use a 7-inch high by 5½-inch wide section of background fabric for the applique and follow instructions in the applique section of this book.

After completing the applique section, proceed with attaching this section to your batting and muslin. Then, continue to fill in remainder of the side with the string method described above. Add lace or trims to edge the applique portion or entire section.

For the **pieced basket effect,** there are four basket weave patterns on pages 9, 10 and 11. Or, use various parts of pieced quilt blocks and/or borders you have enjoyed using in the past. You may either vary the size of the basket to fit your pattern or use the standard 6-inch x 24-inch we have established. If you use the standard 6 by 24 size . . . first piece the side of the basket, then add an 8-inch by 26-inch layer of batting and a layer of muslin backing. Quilt the side and proceed to the instructions on basket construction.

The all-time favorite of many quilters is the **log cabin pattern.** It is also ideal for a basket side (see log cabin basket pictured on the cover). Size of the log templates may be determined from the pattern illustrated on page 7.

Basket pictured is 6 inches square. To make it, piece four log cabin blocks for the sides using the quilt-as-you-go method. You may use either another log cabin or a 6-inch square plain fabric bottom.

Cut your batting and muslin backing 7 inches square. Make your template from the pattern page and add ¼-inch seam allowance to each log. Next, center piece No. 1 on the batting and backing right side up . . . baste to hold in place.

Add piece No. 2 (with right sides together), stitch ¼-inch seam allowance, lay piece No. 3 in place over Nos. 1 and 2, and stitch. Follow with No. 4, then No. 5, and so on until the square is completed. Each time you have added a log you are stitching through fabric, batting and backing . . . subsequently you will have one quilted basket side when you have added all the pieces (logs). Make the other sides of the basket in the same manner as described above.

The **triangle basket** may be used as a Christmas card holder (pictured on the cover). Triangle template is on the pattern page. This pattern would be the one to use to make your basket flare out at the top.

Piece two sides of the basket together with five triangles on the bottom row and seven on the top row (as drawn on the pattern page). Quilt. For the ends of this particular basket and the bottom, use a single section of fabric rather than piecing triangles. The end section is approximately 3 inches wide plus seam allowance and as high as your triangles turned out to be.

Bottom section needs to be the same 3 inches with seam allowance and as long as the triangles are at the bottom. Cut batting and muslin backing the same size for sides and bottom.

You will find it easier to piece separate side and bottom sections rather than cutting one section of fabric. Additionally, the seams at the bottom provide a firmer support for the basket to sit erect . . . which is required because of the flaring out at the top.

The **puff or bisquit basket** provides a soft, rounded basket feeling. Two different size puffs were used in the example pictured to give a more realistic basket effect. You may choose to vary the size and height of your basket by making three rows the same size or adding a second small row. Templates for both size puffs are on the pattern page.

For each puff, cut the smaller pattern from muslin and the larger pattern from your outside print or a solid fabric. Sew the two together (muslin and right side up-fabric edge together) . . . taking a tuck in the center to make the ends come out even. Stitch one side with ¼-inch seam allowance, then a second side, then a third side . . . leaving the sewing machine needle down in the fabric at the end of the third side corner. Open the fourth unstitched side and stuff a small piece of batting, then continue stitching the fourth side closed. Continue in this manner until you have the required number of puffs.

Using the ¼-inch seam allowance, fold right sides puff to puff and stitch together to form a row. Make another row or rows. Sew rows together until you have the desired size for your basket side.

Flower petal basket may be made by making individual petals of a flower (pattern illustrated on page 8). Cut six outside fabric petals, six lining petals and six batting petals from the pattern. If your batting is not sufficiently stiff, use a section of stiffer pelon as well for reinforcement.

With right sides of the fabric together, batting down towards the sewing machine and pelon to top, stitch around this petal leaving the turning hole at the base open. Turn. Topstitch ¼-inch around the entire flower petal for reinforcing. Now, arrange these petals around the circle (overlap when necessary to fit). Stitch with batting and pelon included. It is a sturdier basket if you tack these petals together near the top. Hand stitch a circle of lining fabric in place. Then, attach your handle to any two petals opposite each other.

Basket Construction

By using one of the above methods, you have your basket side ready to put together. Trim away any excess batting and backing.

Your side piece is also your pattern for the lining. Since the inside diameter of your basket will be smaller than the outside, cut the lining ¼-inch smaller all the way around. Next, sew this rectangle together to form a circle . . . making sure horizontal strips or the continuity of your pattern remains intact.

Now, determine the bottom size circle, oval, rectangle or square you need for your basket. A pattern has not been given for any of the different shaped bottoms since your completed basket size may vary. Drawing tools (compass, straight edge, etc.) are usually recommended to achieve a circle or oval pattern, but it does not have to be that difficult or take a mathematician to figure out.

Simply use your everyday lunch or dinner plates for circles. Small oval platters are ideal for oval patterns. Square patterns can be determined by dividing 4 into the number of inches your basket is in circumference.

Turn plate upside down onto work surface and place basket ring on top of plate. The correct plate size will be one you can visually see about ¼-inch overlap all the way around. This ¼-inch is your seam allowance. Trace around the plate to construct a paper pattern.

Cut muslin, batting, basket's outside bottom fabric and the lining fabric from this circle, oval, or square pattern . . . cutting the lining at least 1/8-inch smaller than the outside fabric. Pin and sew all three bottom pieces (muslin, batting, and outside fabric) together ¼-inch from outer edge to hold in place.

Fold circle in half, then in half again . . . you now have your bottom section quartered. Pin or clip a notch to mark the quarter sections. By folding in half, then half again, mark the quarter sections on your basket side. Match quarter notches on bottom and side, pin baste together prior to sewing. Sew with an ample ¼-inch seam.

Quarter notch the lining bottom and the lining sides and sew three-quarters around the lining bottom to the side. Do not sew the remaining quarter to allow for a turning hole after the basket is attached to the lining.

When making a **ruffle top basket,** the ruffle must be made and attached prior to adding the lining. Cut a section of fabric 4½ inches high by 45 inches wide (width of fabric). Then, fold in half and press. Sew selvage edges together to form a circle. Next, run a gathering thread about ¼-inch from the raw edge.

Gather the ruffle until it is about the size your basket is in circumference. Spread gathers evenly. After stitching the basket side together, stitch ruffle to basket before attaching the lining. If something is required to create a more finished appearance, use eyelet lace or cording to finish off the top edge.

Handle Variations

Handles require special construction and consideration. First decide what type of handle would be best for your basket . . . a plain coordinating fabric handle with possible trim or lace, a braided handle, a stuffed handle, and so on.

For a straight fabric handle, cut your outside basket fabric 4 inches wide by 18 inches long, a backing fabric, and a section of batting 2 inches by 18 inches. Fold the outside and backing fabric together with right sides facing and with batting down towards the sewing machine. Stitch down lengthways ¼-inch, turn inside out using a safety pin to pull the fabric through or the string sewn-in-end method.

Press lightly, then top stitch ¼-inch from each outside edge; if you wish, you may top stitch down the center. This reinforces and makes a handle that is better able to stand up. A handle longer than 18 inches is too long to stand up properly. If your handle tends to droop, try shortening it to 14 inches. Lace or trim may be added as you topstitch.

For the braided handle, cut three sections of fabric 2 inches by 14 inches and three sections of batting 1 inch by 14 inches. The weight of the three pieces requires a little shorter handle.

Fold right sides together with batting on bottom, stitch and turn as before. Stitch across the ends of the three pieces . . . anchor them under the presser foot of your sewing machine . . . then braid together until all three ends meet at the opposite end of your braiding. Machine stitch across ends to hold together until you sew handle into position on the basket.

Stuffed handle is a 4-inch by 14-inch section of fabric. With right sides together, sew ½-inch lengthwise. Turn. Stuff batting in the handle until it is firm (not popping out the seams) . . . leaving the very last ½-inch on each end for sewing closed.

If you would like a shirred fabric stuffed handle, make stuffed handle as described above, then cut a section of fabric 4½ inches by 24 inches, sew together with ¼-inch seam allowance, turn and pull over padded handle arranging shirring. Stitch at end. Machine stitch closed before attaching handle to your basket.

Now that you have your handle ready, let us go **back to basket construction.** Pin the handle on one side, go underneath the basket and match the handle equally halfway around and pin it to the other side. With right sides together, slip the lining up and over the bottom of the basket and pin baste around the top edge. Sew ¼-inch completely around the top.

Double check to make sure the fabric is caught all the way around with an ample seam allowance. This is important to prevent any stitching from pulling out.

Turn basket inside out through the opening left in the lining. Stitch opening closed. To hold the lining down inside the basket and to reinforce the top, topstitch down ¼-inch through all thicknesses completely around the top edge. This also reinforces the handle and helps it to stand up better. Additionally, topstitching 1/8-inch through all thicknesses up from the bottom seam gives the bottom added firmness.

Pictures of an actual basket in construction are presented as a visual aid. Try making one basket, then a second. It's fun!

Preparing string side.

Cut lining ¼-inch less than basket side all the way around.

Determine bottom size with plate or compass.

Cut bottom outside, muslin, lining and batting.

Notch bottom and sides. Match notches, pin and sew bottom.

Make handle.

With handle under basket, lining and basket right sides together, slide lining up and over basket, then sew.

Topstitch top and bottom.

Log Cabin

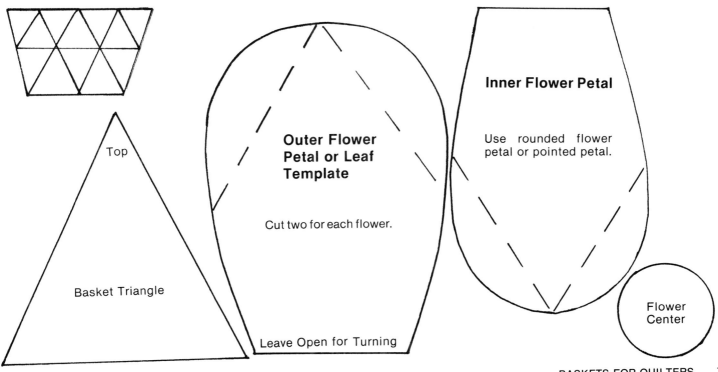

				13
			9	
		5		
	1	2		
4	3	6		
8	7	10		
12				11

Use template as:
A. Individual log template (add seam allowance)
B. Sewing guide (as 1 to 2 to 3)
C. Full size as backing template with 1-inch for seam allowance (trim excess after sewing)
D. Bottom of basket template
E. Lining for basket template (cut 1/4-inch smaller than full square)

Top

Basket Triangle

Outer Flower Petal or Leaf Template

Cut two for each flower.

Leave Open for Turning

Inner Flower Petal

Use rounded flower petal or pointed petal.

Flower Center

Larger Puff
Cut 8 per row for 20-inch finished piece

Muslin backing template

Smaller Puff
Cut 16 per row for 20-inch piece

Muslin backing template

Circle Bottom for Petal Basket
Cut 1 outside fabric, 1 batting, 1 pelon and 1 lining

Stitch around edge

Stitch around edge

Petal Template for Petal Basket
Cut 6 outside fabric, 6 lining, 6 batting and 6 pelon

Leave open for turning.

Applique Designs

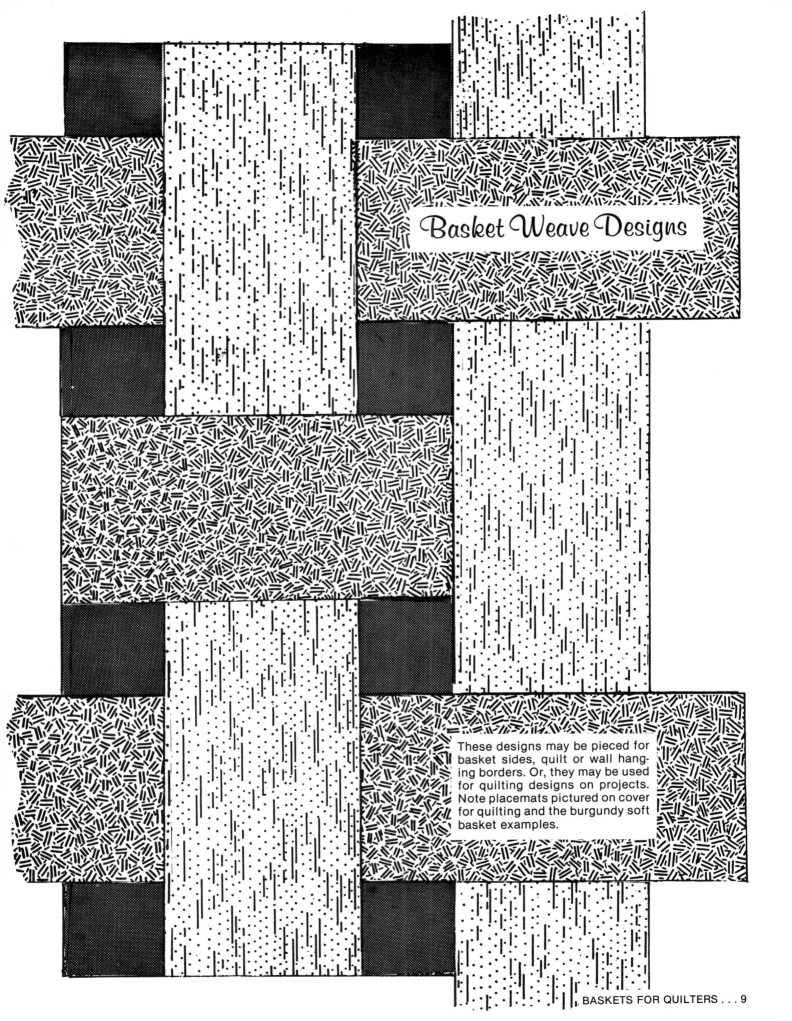

Basket Weave Designs

These designs may be pieced for basket sides, quilt or wall hanging borders. Or, they may be used for quilting designs on projects. Note placemats pictured on cover for quilting and the burgundy soft basket examples.

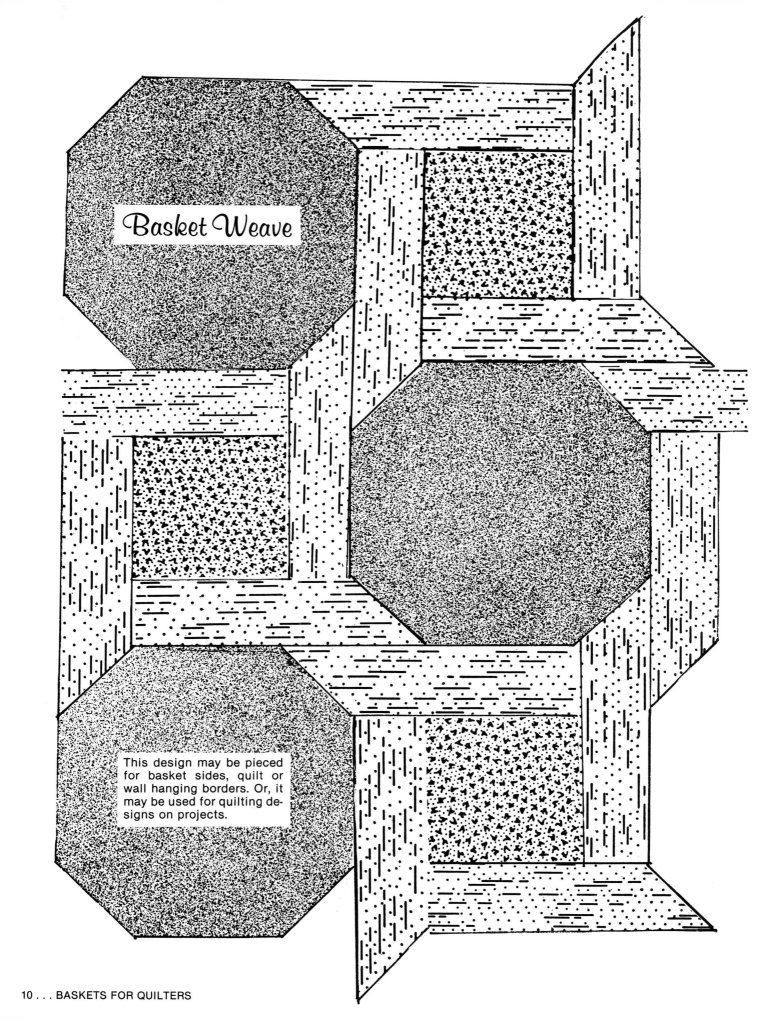

Basket Weave

This design may be pieced for basket sides, quilt or wall hanging borders. Or, it may be used for quilting designs on projects.

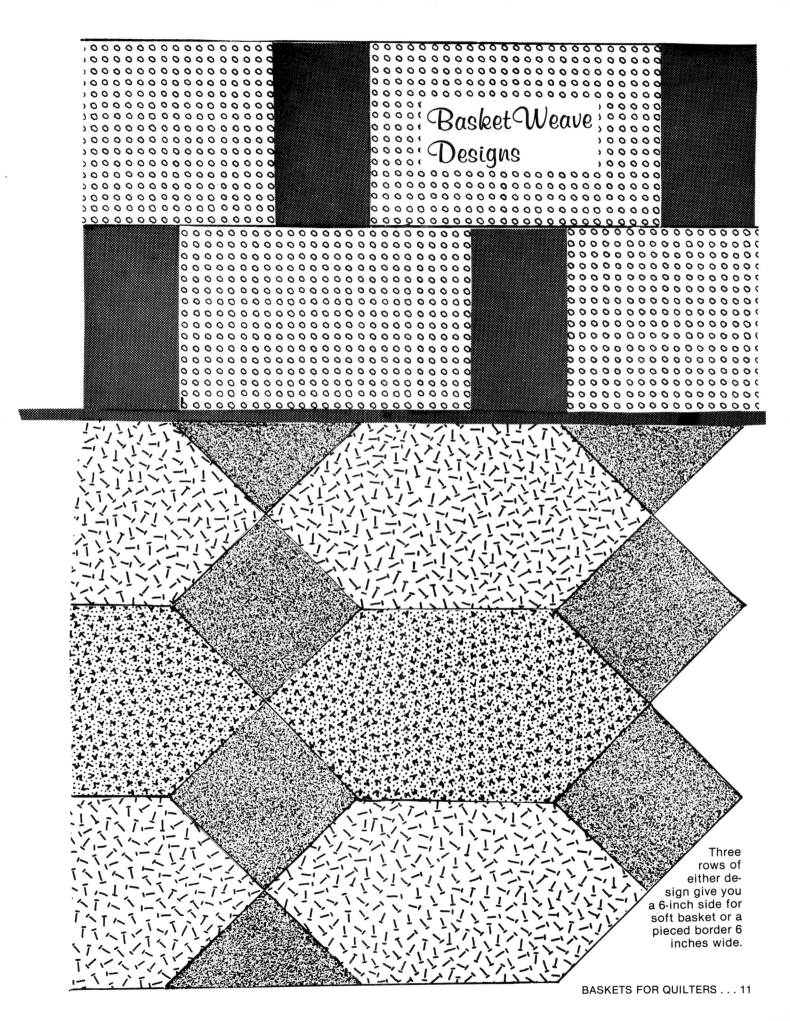

Basket Weave Designs

Three rows of either design give you a 6-inch side for soft basket or a pieced border 6 inches wide.

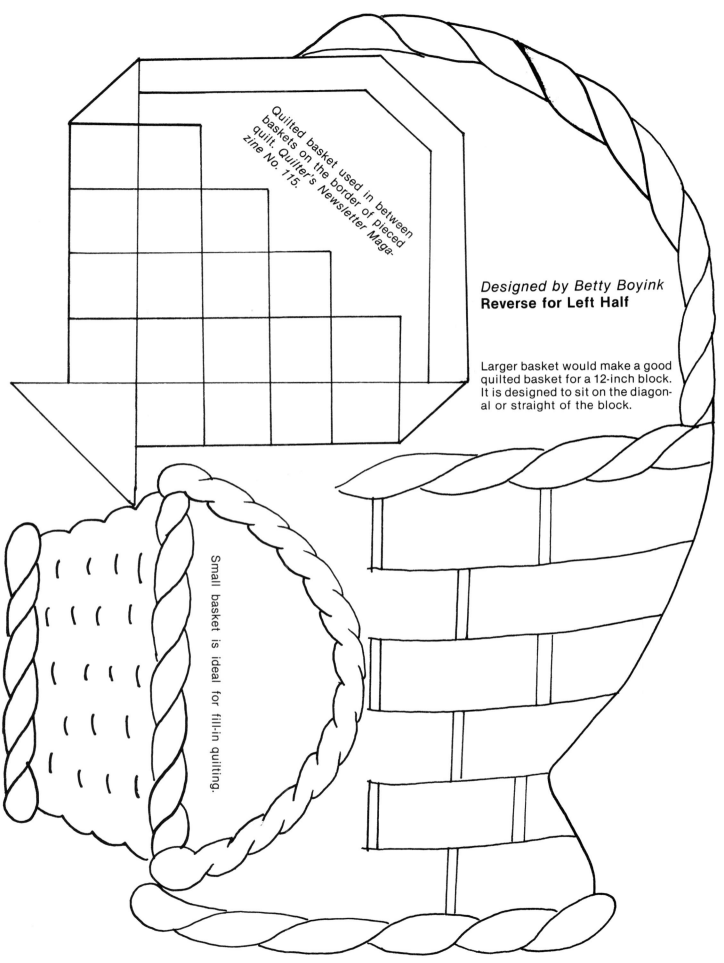

Quilted basket used in between baskets on the border of pieced quilt. Quilter's Newsletter Magazine No. 115.

Designed by Betty Boyink
Reverse for Left Half

Larger basket would make a good quilted basket for a 12-inch block. It is designed to sit on the diagonal or straight of the block.

Small basket is ideal for fill-in quilting.

Pieced Baskets

A book about baskets would not be complete without some pieced basket templates for piecing and quilting individual pillows, totes, wall hangings, quilts or similar items.

The next few pages are devoted to 20 different, mostly pieced baskets. The "mostly" refers to the fact that some of the baskets have appliqued handles. Quilt pictured on the cover provides an idea of how these patterns might be used.

Center medallion basket is an 18-inch star flower basket block squared off with the bottom half of the orange basket block. Basket was elongated to a rectangular shape to accommodate one of the larger style beds. Four postage stamp baskets were placed at either end.

Fourteen 12-inch basket blocks surround the medallion section. A different pattern was selected for each block.

Border is made up of the smaller postage stamp basket. It is a relatively easy basket to make just the right size to fit the border length and width.

The quilt pictured does not include baskets that are both pieced and appliqued. For the most part, the baskets were not adorned with applique flowers, fruit, and so on to ensure that the basket itself was the predominant focal point.

Basket patterns are ideal for developing your own designs and ideas. For example, select the bottom portion of a basket from the pieced section of this book, then turn to the applique section and select a top arrangement. Or, another great quilt idea would be to use the various flowers as realistic as possible along with a pieced basket. I guess Ruby McKim said it best in her book *101 Patchwork Patterns*, "There is no one way to combine colors, to piece or to quilt, and your idea may be as right as another."

4, 8 and 12-Inch Sizes

As you turn the pages, you will find that all baskets are illustrated as a whole block in a 4-inch size. This permits using the illustration as a pattern for a Christmas tree ornament, or in miniature (two of the placemats pictured on the cover utilized the 4-inch size).

All patterns are also depicted in an 8-inch size. These baskets are ideally suited for small quilt blocks, baby quilts, tooth fairy pillows, wall hangings, placemats, the bib on an apron of a garment, and skirt or jacket pockets. 8-inch diagonally set basket blocks may be squared off by piecing in four corner triangles to increase the block size to 11¼ inches . . . giving you just the right size for certain projects.

Additionally, 12-inch patterns are included to provide you with the most popular quilt block size. This size is also easily adaptable to pillows, totes, and similar quilt projects.

New Designs

Upright basket designs are few and far between. Sampler quilt pictured on the cover includes two traditional designs: **rose bud basket** with appliqued handle and **colonial basket** of triangles with a very distinguishable appliqued handle. Since other traditional basket blocks were similar to these two designs, two original patterns were created: named diamond basket and jewel basket.

Diamond Basket has a pieced handle of squares, but may also have the top half a solid fabric with an appliqued handle (see the bell pull on the cover for this variation). If a size other than the 4, 8 or 12-inch illustrated is required, this basket may be grafted by dividing the total square into sixths. Basket part and handle part split the square in two equal sections.

Jewel Basket with applique handle was named because of the simulated jewel setting with a lighter color fabric highlighting the diamond center. To graph, simply divide the entire square into fifths.

Changing Block Sizes

Perhaps you need a different size block than the 4, 8 or 12-inch illustrated. It is really quite easy to change the size of the block to the exact size you require.

Blocks are identified by either 4, 5, 6, 7 or 8 patch. To obtain your finished block size, you may use either graph paper or the paper folding method to arrive at the number of units across a block.

To use the **paper folding method** of determining your pattern, take a square of paper the size of the block you desire and fold it into an equal number of sections corresponding to the number of patches in the original block pattern. Unfold the paper and measure from the edge of the paper to the first fold. Mark off this measurement completely around the outer edge of the paper. (If you attach a piece of masking tape on a ruler, you will find this step easier to do.)

Now, lightly graph across the paper drawing lines from top to bottom and from left to right connecting the marks you previously made. Remember all patterns illustrated in this book are depicted in a 4-inch block. Use this 4-inch block as a guide to draw in the design on the lightly graphed paper you have just made.

For quilters making a basket sampler quilt, 4, 5, 6, 7 and 8 patch baskets are included. You will discover that it is easiest to select and do all the same patch baskets (i.e., 4 or 5, etc.) at one sitting since many of the templates are interchangeable. This eliminates making duplicate templates.

A rectangular basket block was also designed especially for this book (page 17). Examples of how this block is used are displayed on the cover (note dolly quilt and picture frame).

If diagonal blocks present a problem for your project, simply add a triangle to each of the four sides to attain an upright basket. When converting diagonal to upright, 4-inch block becomes 5-5/8 inches square, 8-inch becomes 11-1/4 inches square, and 12-inch becomes 16-1/2 inches square.

Since many projects require a 12-inch block, an ideal solution is to enlarge the 8-inch pattern to 8½ inches, then add the four triangles to the diagonal pattern to produce a standard 12-inch upright basket block.

Fabric Yardages

Since there are so many variables, yardage for your basket quilt must be figured on an individual basis. A suggested way to figure yardage is to determine how many pieces of a particular template are required, then add up the number of pieces that will fit across the prewashed fabric. It is always a good idea to add a little extra for insurance. Continue in this manner for each template.

For quilters possessing a great deal of temerity . . . especially ones with husbands that constantly ask, "Why do you have so much fabric around here?" . . . you might use the "catch-as-catch-can" method of yardage figuring. This method was used for the basket medallion sampler quilt shown on the cover.

One-half to one yard pieces of coordinating fabrics were purchased for the basket blocks. A few 2-yard pieces were thrown in for stripping or inner borders. Then, a 3-yard piece was tossed on the fabric store's cutting table for the outer borders. That's it — catch-as-catch-can.

For the adventuresome, this method might turn a dull routine into a more creative design. In fact, some of this writer's more interesting projects have turned out to be attractively distinctive because of the fabric yardage on hand.

A final suggestion regarding yardage would be that when you return home from the fabric store immediately wash the fabric, cut out all the blocks required, then store all the pieces for each block in a separate sandwich baggie.

Even though you have the best of intentions to put your quilt top together promptly, the bagged bits and pieces might somehow find their way into the hands of one of your granddaughters. A discovery of this type by one of your granddaughters . . . with everything for each block together or a whole quilt top in a larger bag . . . can be almost as good as passing on an heirloom quilt.

As a teacher and designer of quilts, students have presented similar challenges with bits and pieces of treasures found in grandmother's attic. Completing these once-forgotten projects linked generations in a spiritual way that could never be achieved with an inherited, finished quilt.

From Patterns to Quilt Top

You have selected the block and/or blocks you want to use, what next?

1. Trace very carefully over the template in the book. A straight edge (draftsmen's triangle or ruler) is recommended for accuracy when tracing straight lines. You may add your ¼-inch seam allowance before making a template or if you prefer, add the ¼-inch seam allowance on the fabric while you are scissoring. Glue this tracing paper template to either sand paper or quilter's transparent plastic for a more permanent template.

2. Lay the template on the fabric and trace around it . . . measuring out ¼-inch entirely around the template for seam allowance (if you have not added it to your template). Templates without seam allowances included will provide pencil lines as sewing guides when pattern is traced onto your fabric.

3. Match two triangles to form a square . . . sewing on marked seam line from corner dot-to-dot.

4. Join squares together to form a row (4-inch block illustrated in this book is your guide). Now, sew rows together to form complete basket unit. Be careful not to bury the points of triangles or have excess of other fabric.

5. Next, add side rectangle units, then add top and base triangles to complete the square.

6. Measure sewn block to check for accuracy, clip excess at intersections and press seam allowances towards the darker fabric. Never press open.

Bias and straight edge of the fabric is the next order of business . . . especially with basket blocks where there are so many triangles. General rule of thumb is that all outside edges of the block must be on the straight edge of the fabric. This will be very important when you assemble your blocks together.

Functional Baskets

Every little girl and even grown-up girls enjoy pockets. Baskets are ideal for pockets on clothing, totes, tooth fairy pillows and so on. Here is how you do it!

First, piece the basket half of the block minus the handle configuration. Next, cut out a solid piece (best to use background fabric) using the pieced section you just put together as your template.

Now, place right sides together and sew across the top maintaining a ¼-inch seam allowance to prevent any burying of the points. Turn and press.

At this point, it is best to quilt your sewn together block. You will find it is much easier to quilt this half section before adding the back of the pocket and top half of the block.

After quilting, you are ready for the top half. Top half consists of top template of the chosen block pattern plus a fabric piece (again, you might use background fabric) sewn to the top half. The fabric piece sewn to the top becomes the back of the pocket. This bottom section of fabric added to the top pattern gives you the full dimensions of the entire block (do not forget seam allowance). Now, add batting and backing. Finish by quilting the top half.

Another option would be to use just the triangle section of the block for a much smaller pocket. This is how one side of the tote pictured on page 50 was done. Basically, it is the same procedure as described above, except instead of the back pocket fabric being the full dimensions of the block it only includes the triangle section.

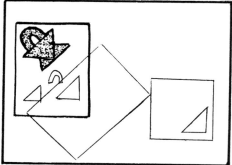

Make template.

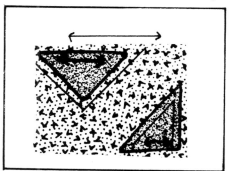

Mark seam allowance on fabric or template.

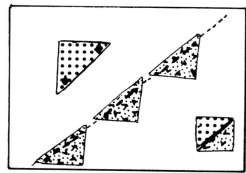

Stitch dot-to-dot or machine stitch in rows.

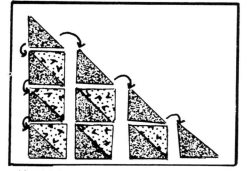

After joining triangles, join square-to-square to form rows.

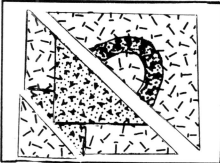

Add top triangle and bottom triangle; or remainder of block.

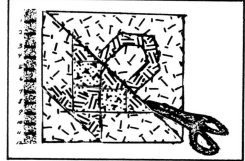

Measure for accuracy, then press seams toward dark fabric. Clip excess seam at points.

Diamond Basket

4, 8 and 12-inch sizes
Six Patch, add seam allowance

Designed by Betty Boyink. Since necessity is the mother of invention, the diamond basket was created to fulfill a need for a straight-up basket pattern rather than a diagonal basket. There are a number of applique baskets that fulfill this requirement, but very few pieced patterns. When using this pattern, be sure to mark center point of small triangles around diamonds (triangles are not equilateral). Both pieced and applique handle variations are illustrated.

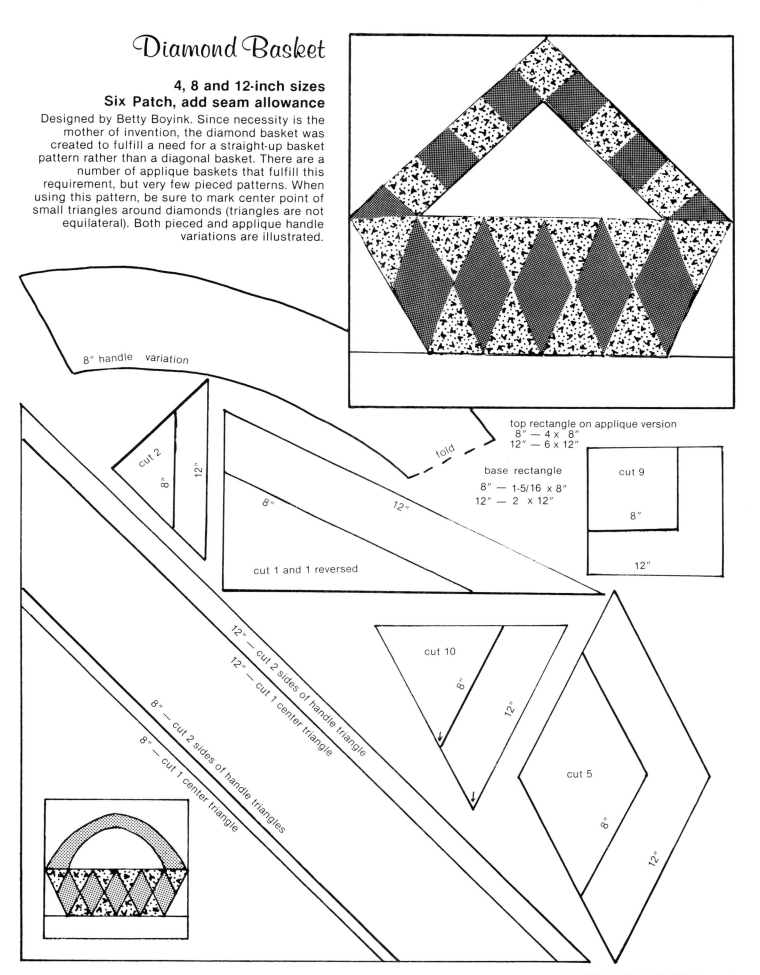

8" handle variation

cut 2
8"
12"

fold

8"
12"
cut 1 and 1 reversed

top rectangle on applique version
8" — 4 x 8"
12" — 6 x 12"

base rectangle
8" — 1-5/16 x 8"
12" — 2 x 12"

cut 9
8"
12"

12" — cut 2 sides of handle triangle
12" — cut 1 center triangle

8" — cut 2 sides of handle triangles
8" — cut 1 center triangle

cut 10
8"
12"

cut 5
8"
12"

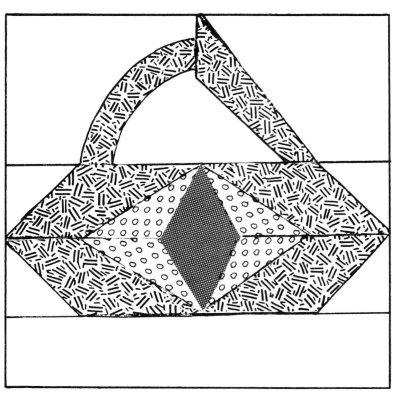

Jewel Basket

4, 8 and 12-inch sizes
Five Patch, add seam allowance

Original design by Betty Boyink. This is a pieced basket with an appliqued handle that sits square on the block. Two handle variations are given, one curved and the other more angular. By choosing the lighter fabrics around the center diamond, a jewel setting effect can be achieved. The lavender and purple pillow grouping pictured on the cover includes this basket.

under basket — background
  8″ — cut 1 — 1-5/8 x 8″
  12″ — cut 1 — 2- 3/8 x 12″

top of block — background
  8″ — cut 1 — 3-1/4 x 8″
  12″ — cut 1 — 4-3/4 x 12″

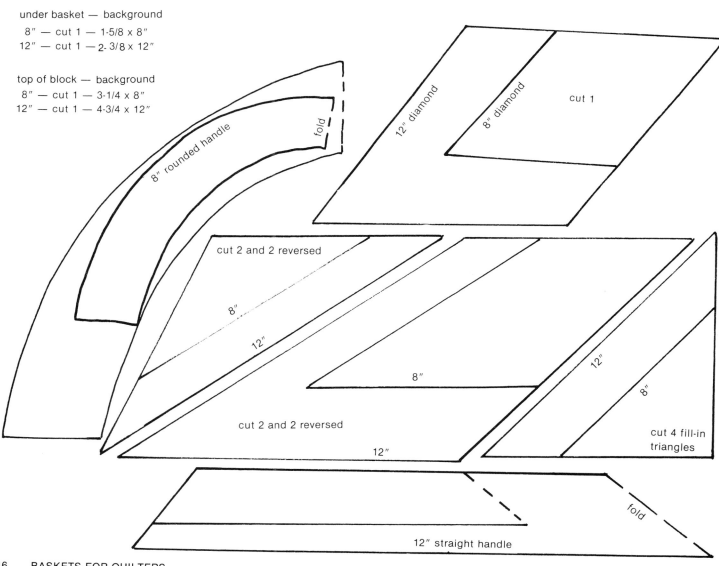

Rectangle Basket

5 x 6 inches and 10 x 12 inches, add seam allowance

Pictured on the cover in the smaller size for the doll's quilt, it is also shown in the 10-inch x 12-inch size for the framed-in-fabric picture. Rectangle blocks permit you to do some interesting designing since the rectangle size needed for a quilt can be easily achieved with the 10-inch x 12-inch pattern . . . seven blocks across by seven blocks down. Quilt size would be 70 x 84, plus border and stripping. A rectangle block might be more flattering used in some clothing.

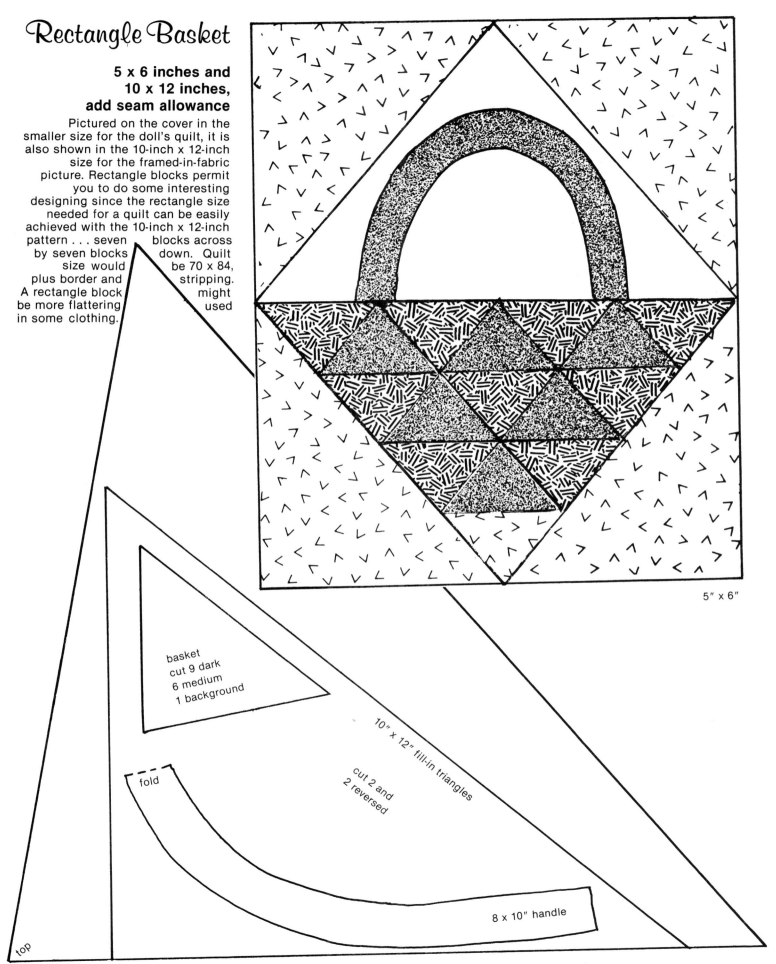

5" x 6"

basket
cut 9 dark
6 medium
1 background

10" x 12" fill-in triangles

cut 2 and
2 reversed

fold

top

8 x 10" handle

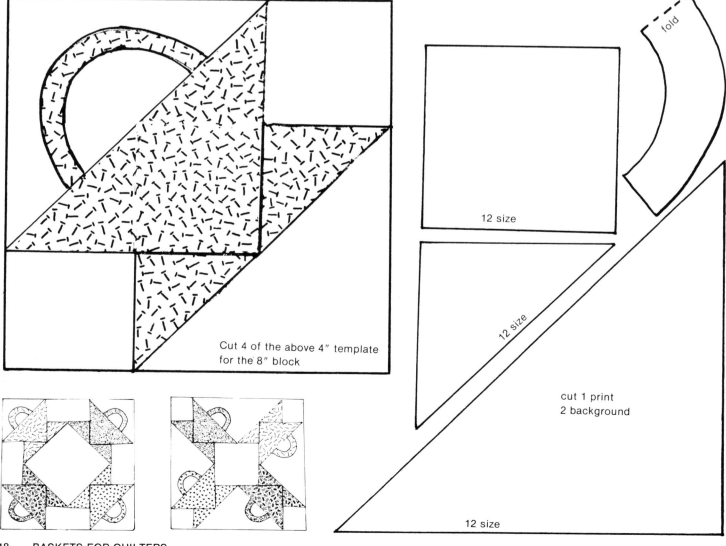

Postage Stamp Basket

4, 8 and 12-inch sizes
Plus 4-inch of individual basket
Three Patch for individual basket
Six Patch for whole block

This quilt stamp block was a part of the American Folk Art Series of stamps and was issued March 8, 1978 as a 13c stamp. The block format was derived from a quilt made in New York City in 1875. "Folk Art, USA and Quilts" as well as "13c" lettering was printed on each of the four baskets.

Because of the simplicity of one individual basket, this is a good pattern to make use of the 4-inch size. A postage stamp pillow is pictured on the cover, individual baskets border the pieced quilt, and coasters (also could be used as tree ornaments) are shown in the table setting with the log cabin basket. Two of the placemats use the 4-inch size. The individual basket block would be a good beginner's block.

Cut 4 of the above 4" template for the 8" block

12 size

fold

12 size

12 size

cut 1 print
2 background

12 size

Variations of a 4-Patch

4, 8 and 12-inch sizes
Four Patch, add seam allowance

An easy block for beginners, this four patch block is pictured in the three potholders on the cover. The 8-inch size is ideal for potholders. Quilt behind the vest photograph uses this block, but only in two colors.

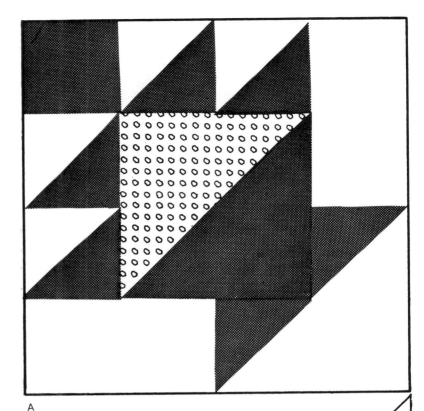

A

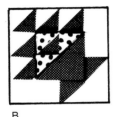

B

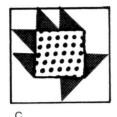

C

Center square of
basket C is
8″ — 4 x 4″
12″ — 6 x 6″

rectangle side
8″ — 2 x 4″
12″ — 3 x 6″

square at top of basket A — 12″

square at top of basket A — 8″

12″ basket and center of A — — — basket of B — 12″

12″ base triangle

8″ basket and center of A — — — basket of B — 8″

8″ base triangle

12″ handle triangle

8″ handle triangle

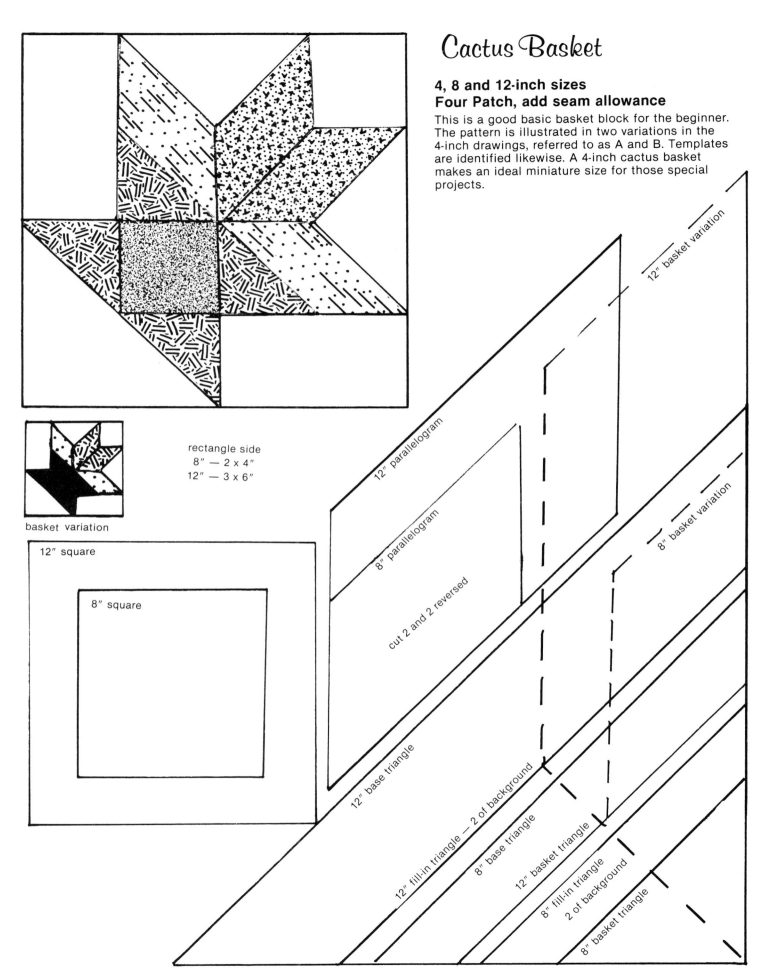

Cactus Basket

4, 8 and 12-inch sizes
Four Patch, add seam allowance

This is a good basic basket block for the beginner. The pattern is illustrated in two variations in the 4-inch drawings, referred to as A and B. Templates are identified likewise. A 4-inch cactus basket makes an ideal miniature size for those special projects.

basket variation

rectangle side
8″ — 2 x 4″
12″ — 3 x 6″

12″ square

8″ square

12″ basket variation

12″ parallelogram

8″ parallelogram

cut 2 and 2 reversed

8″ basket variation

12″ base triangle

12″ fill-in triangle — 2 of background

8″ base triangle

12″ basket triangle

8″ fill-in triangle 2 of background

8″ basket triangle

Bread Basket

4, 8 and 12-inch sizes
Four Patch, add seam allowance

Illustrated are two variations of this simpler of the basket patterns. The tea cozy pictured on the cover uses this 8-inch pattern with just the two added triangles at the base to square off the bottom only. An apron makes use of the other version for pockets and is shown on page 50. Be sure to follow templates for A or B using the 4-inch and 1-inch guide.

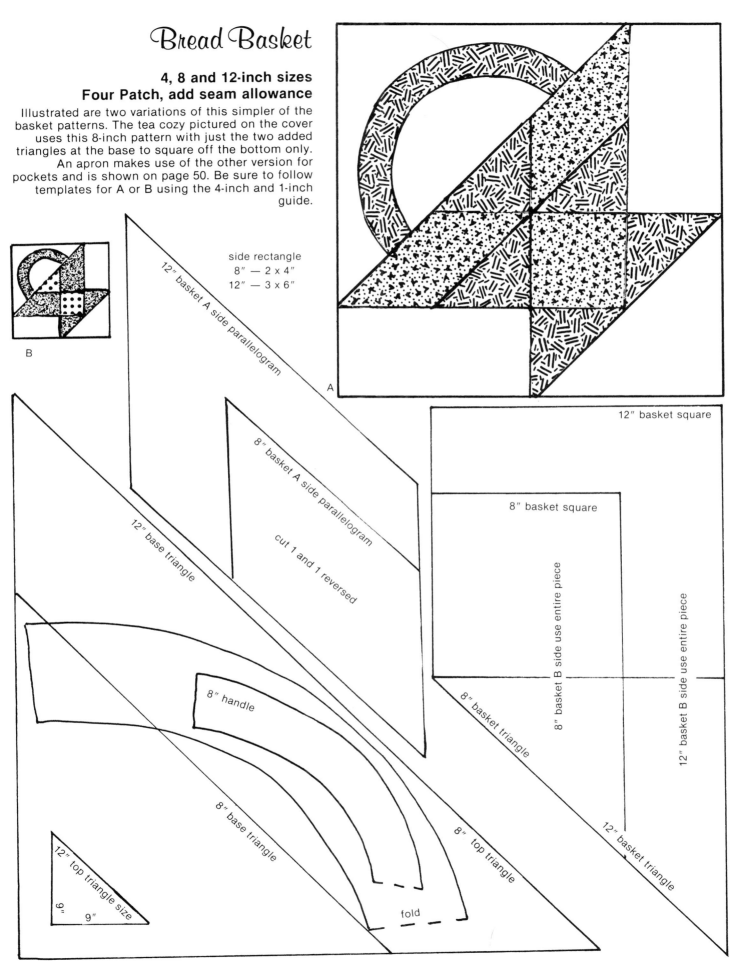

B

side rectangle
8" — 2 x 4"
12" — 3 x 6"

A

12" basket A side parallelogram

8" basket A side parallelogram

cut 1 and 1 reversed

12" basket square

8" basket square

8" basket B side use entire piece

12" basket B side use entire piece

12" base triangle

8" handle

8" base triangle

8" basket triangle

8" top triangle

12" basket triangle

12" top triangle size
9"   9"

fold

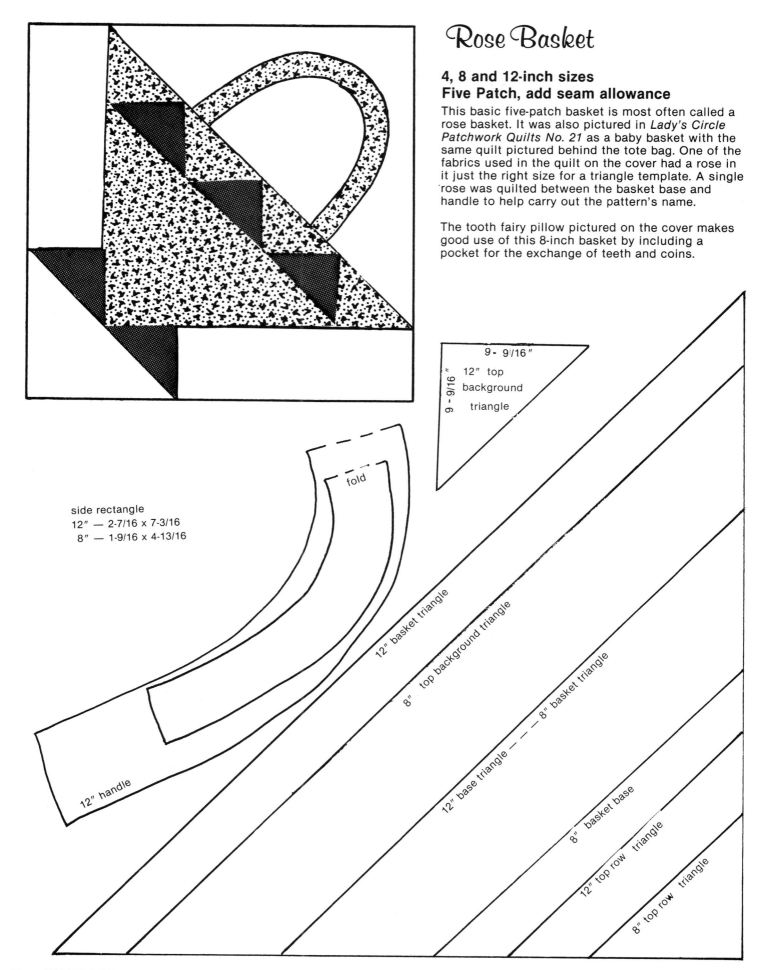

Rose Basket

4, 8 and 12-inch sizes
Five Patch, add seam allowance

This basic five-patch basket is most often called a rose basket. It was also pictured in *Lady's Circle Patchwork Quilts No. 21* as a baby basket with the same quilt pictured behind the tote bag. One of the fabrics used in the quilt on the cover had a rose in it just the right size for a triangle template. A single rose was quilted between the basket base and handle to help carry out the pattern's name.

The tooth fairy pillow pictured on the cover makes good use of this 8-inch basket by including a pocket for the exchange of teeth and coins.

9 - 9/16″

9 - 9/16″

12″ top background triangle

side rectangle
12″ — 2-7/16 x 7-3/16
8″ — 1-9/16 x 4-13/16

fold

12″ basket triangle

8″ top background triangle

12″ base triangle — — — 8″ basket triangle

8″ basket base

12″ top row triangle

8″ top row triangle

12″ handle

Grape Basket
Fruit Basket

4, 8 and 12-inch sizes
Five Patch, add seam allowance

Both the grape and fruit baskets are basic five patch blocks and relatively easy for a beginning piecer. Many of the same pattern pieces are utilized in each basket. The fruit basket, with its open space under the pieced handle, is ideal for quilters that prefer quilting space. The table runner features the grape basket.

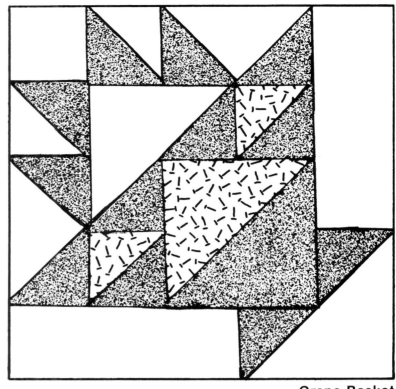

Fruit Basket

Grape Basket

side rectangle
8" — 1-9/16 x 4-13/16
12" — 2-7/16 x 7-3/16

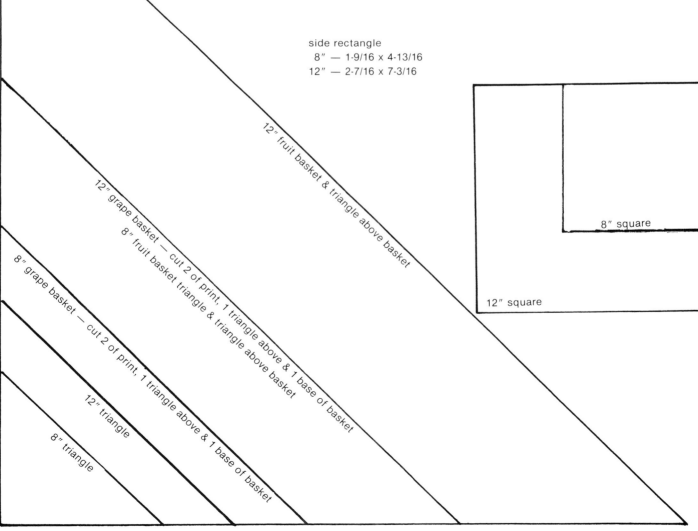

12" fruit basket & triangle above basket

12" grape basket — cut 2 of print, 1 triangle above & 1 base of basket

8" fruit basket triangle & triangle above basket

8" grape basket — cut 2 of print, 1 triangle above & 1 base of basket

12" triangle

8" triangle

8" square

12" square

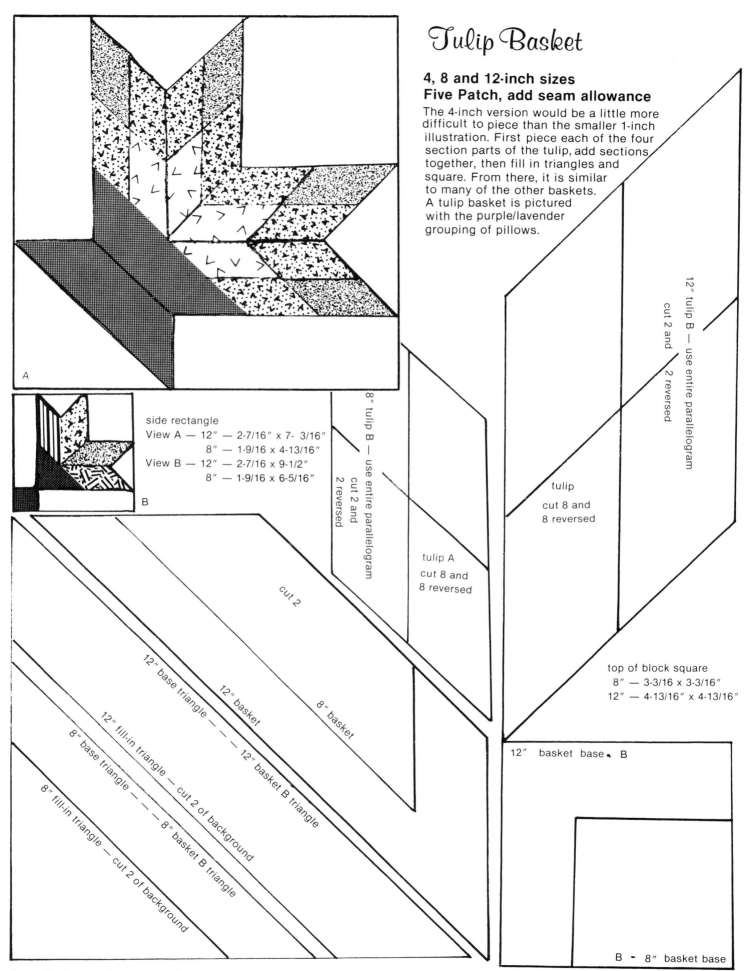

Tulip Basket

4, 8 and 12-inch sizes
Five Patch, add seam allowance

The 4-inch version would be a little more difficult to piece than the smaller 1-inch illustration. First piece each of the four section parts of the tulip, add sections together, then fill in triangles and square. From there, it is similar to many of the other baskets. A tulip basket is pictured with the purple/lavender grouping of pillows.

A

B

side rectangle
View A — 12" — 2-7/16" x 7- 3/16"
　　　　　8" — 1-9/16 x 4-13/16"
View B — 12" — 2-7/16 x 9-1/2"
　　　　　8" — 1-9/16 x 6-5/16"

8" tulip B — use entire parallelogram
cut 2 and
2 reversed

12" tulip B — use entire parallelogram
cut 2 and 2 reversed

tulip
cut 8 and
8 reversed

tulip A
cut 8 and
8 reversed

cut 2

12" base triangle — — — 12" basket B triangle

12" basket

8" basket

12" fill-in triangle — cut 2 of background

8" base triangle — — — 8" basket B triangle

8" fill-in triangle — cut 2 of background

top of block square
8" — 3-3/16 x 3-3/16"
12" — 4-13/16" x 4-13/16"

12" basket base - B

B - 8" basket base

𝓛𝓮𝓪𝓯𝔂 𝓑𝓪𝓼𝓴𝓮𝓽

4, 8 and 12-inch sizes
Five Patch, add seam allowance

A little more difficult basket and not for the beginning piecer. Research established this pattern originating in the early 1930's. October 1979 issue of *Quilter's Newsletter Magazine* also had an excellent feature article on the pattern in its "OLD-TIME QUILTING" highlights. An intriguing pattern, it has a most unusual basket setting occupying not quite half the block and a very unusual pointed top.

12"   8"

cut 1 and 1 reversed background

8" — broken lines within each 12" template
broken lines not seam allowance markings

12" basket triangle

8" basket triangle

cut 6 dark
& 10 light

outside leaf

cut 1 and
1 reversed

cut 1 and
1 reversed
background

center leaf
cut 1

place on fold

fold

8"

8"

8"

12"

12"

12"

cut 1 and
1 reversed
background

mid-leaf

cut 1 and
1 reversed

8"   12"

8"

cut 1 and
1 reversed
background

12"

8"

12"

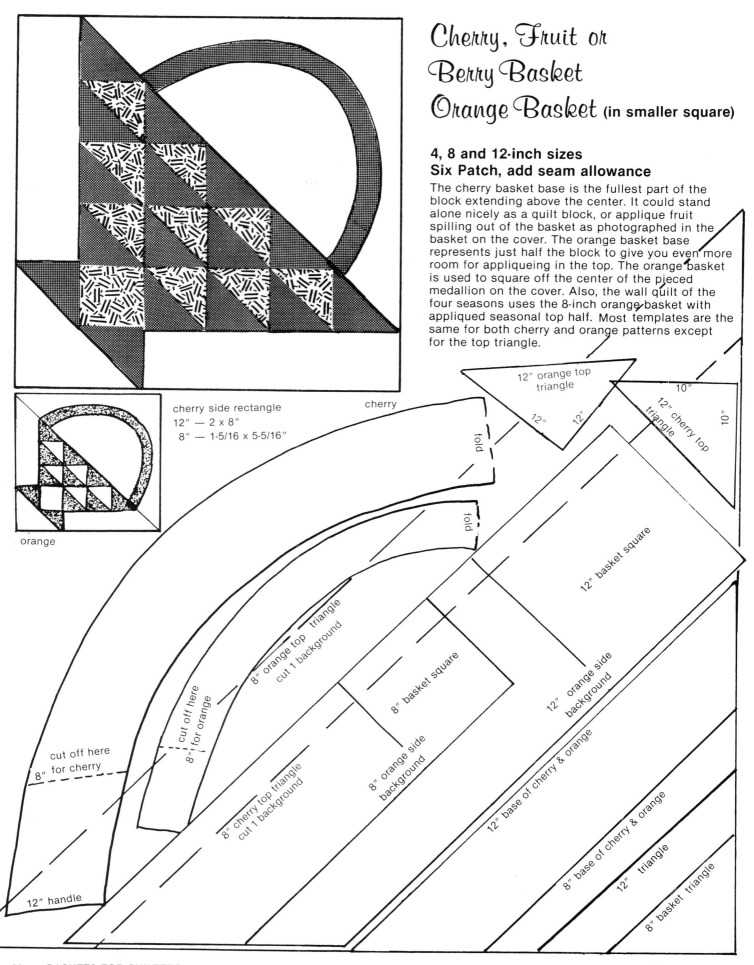

Cherry, Fruit or Berry Basket Orange Basket (in smaller square)

4, 8 and 12-inch sizes
Six Patch, add seam allowance

The cherry basket base is the fullest part of the block extending above the center. It could stand alone nicely as a quilt block, or applique fruit spilling out of the basket as photographed in the basket on the cover. The orange basket base represents just half the block to give you even more room for appliqueing in the top. The orange basket is used to square off the center of the pieced medallion on the cover. Also, the wall quilt of the four seasons uses the 8-inch orange basket with appliqued seasonal top half. Most templates are the same for both cherry and orange patterns except for the top triangle.

cherry

cherry side rectangle
12" — 2 x 8"
8" — 1-5/16 x 5-5/16"

orange

fold

fold

12" orange top triangle

12"

12"

10"

12" cherry top triangle

10"

12" basket square

8" orange top triangle
cut 1 background

8" basket square

12" orange side background

cut off here
8" for orange

8" orange side background

12" base of cherry & orange

cut off here
8" for cherry

8" cherry top triangle
cut 1 background

12" base of cherry & orange

8" base of cherry & orange

12" triangle

8" basket triangle

12" handle

Checkerboard Basket

4, 8 and 12-inch sizes
Six Patch, add seam allowance

Quilt Almanac 1982 uses the checkerboard bottom basket with the top variation. See the clothing page for this basket used on the back of the string vest, and the cover for the top variation in the purple/lavender pillow grouping. This is a good diagonal basket for quilters that do not like applique well enough to even tack down a handle. It is totally pieced! Sometimes the variation goes by different names.

Use side of basket template from orange basket (page 26)

checkerboard basket base

12" handle

cut 2

8" handle

12" under handle triangle

8" under handle triangle — — base of 12" basket

base of 8" basket

12" triangle

8" triangle

fold

8" square

12" square

8" side of background

12" side of background

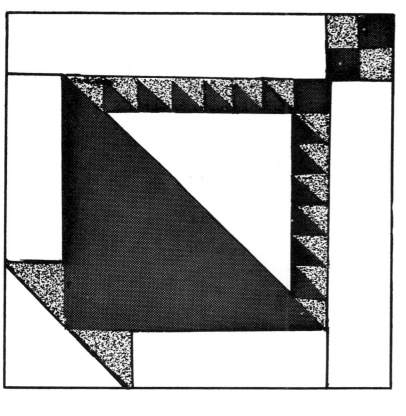

Hanging Basket

4, 8 and 12-inch sizes
Six Patch, add seam allowance

This pattern was published in the *Kansas City Star* newspaper in 1937 and was also listed in Barbara Brackman's *Encyclopedia of Pieced Blocks.* It has some of the qualities of a quilter's macrame handle basket. Because of the delicate triangles of the handle, it would be easier to use in the 8-inch or 12-inch size.

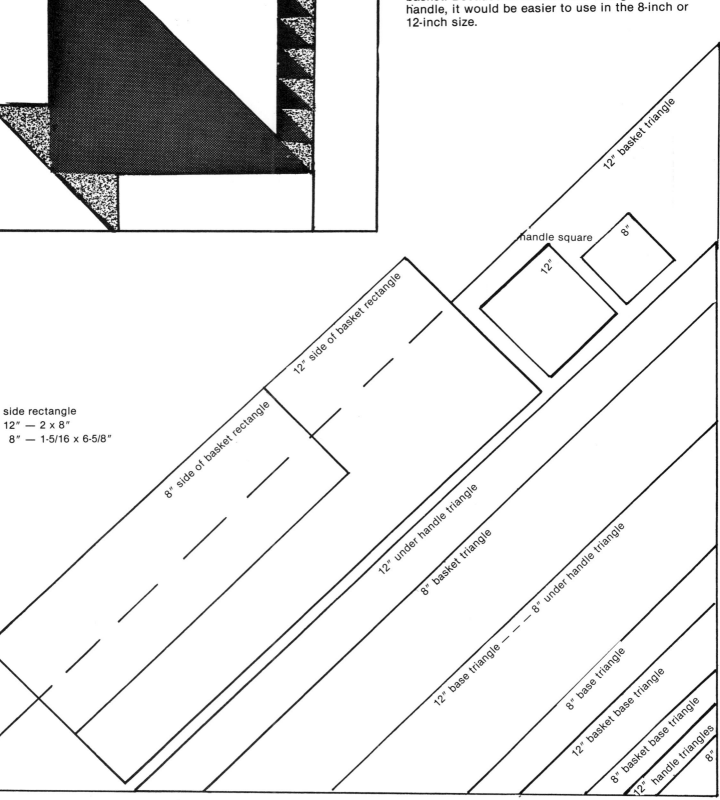

side rectangle
12" — 2 x 8"
8" — 1-5/16 x 6-5/8"

Friendship Basket

4, 8 and 12-inch sizes
Six Patch, add seam allowance

There are friendship blocks of many variations, from Dresden plate, album and on and on . . . so why not a basket block designed especially for use as a friendship block? This is an *Old Chelsea Station Needlecraft Service* pattern from the 1930's.

There is no friend like an old friend
Who has shared our morning days;
no greeting like his welcome,
no homage like his praise.
Fame is the scentless sunflower
with gaudy crown·of gold,
But Friendship is the breathing rose
with sweets in every fold.
Author Unknown — discovered on
an old cross stitch sampler

A suggested use of this block might be to embroider the above poem in the four parallel bars of the basket for a gift to a dear friend. The green friendship pillow on the cover was done in all solid fabrics to provide plenty of room for names of a local quilt group.

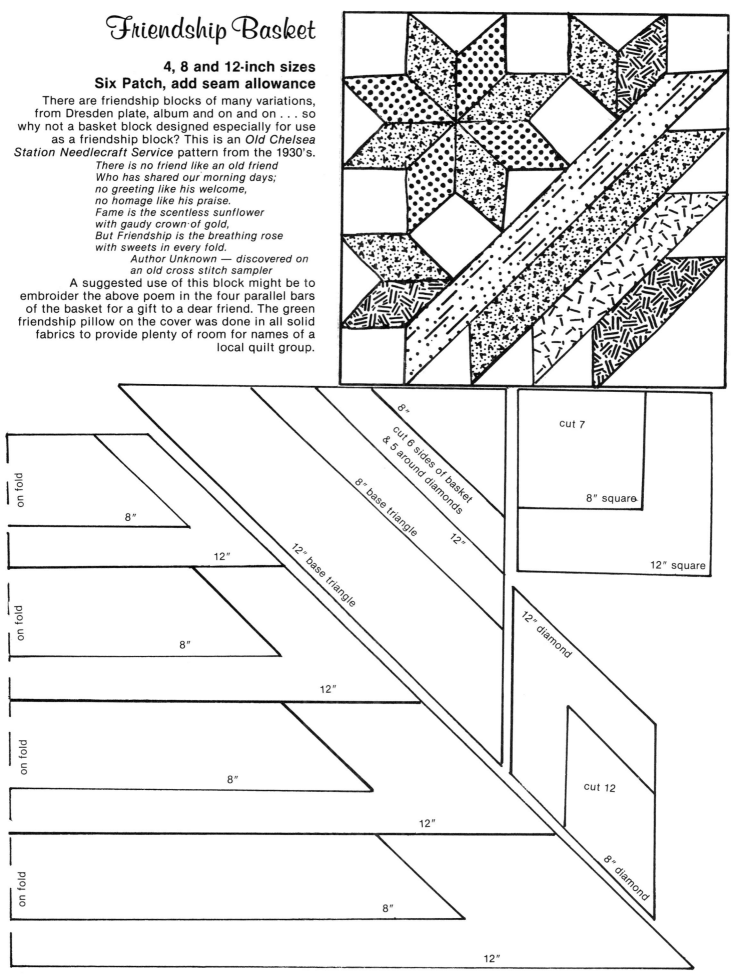

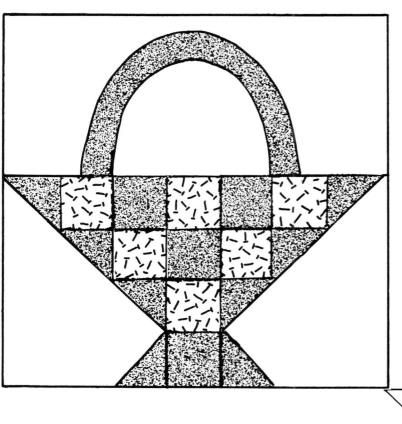

Rosebud Basket

4, 8 and 12-inch sizes
Seven Patch, add seam allowance

One of the few baskets that sits square on the block, subsequently it has many advantages. This 8-inch size was used in one of the tooth fairy pillows as an actual pocket basket. Instructions are in the pieced section. Some patterns like this one have appliqued points along the top of the basket for a rosebud effect. The bib of the apron pictured on page 50 makes use of the 8-inch rosebud basket as a pocket.

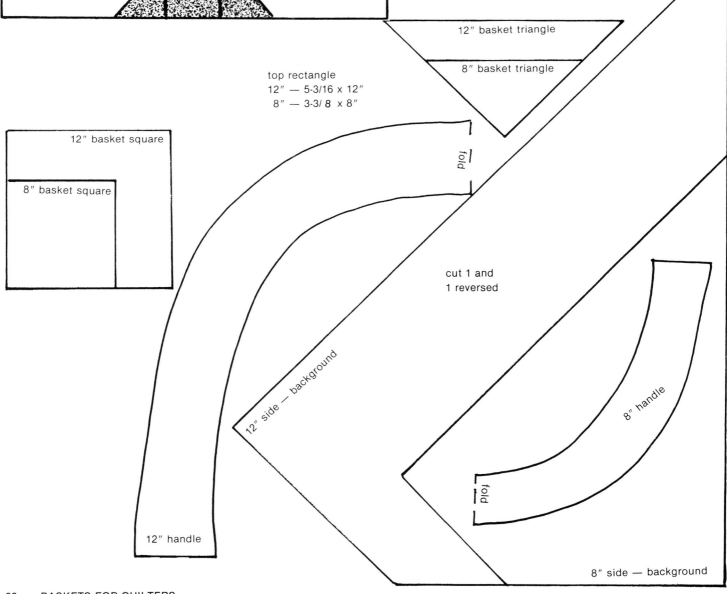

12″ basket triangle

8″ basket triangle

top rectangle
12″ — 5-3/16 x 12″
8″ — 3-3/8 x 8″

fold

12″ basket square

8″ basket square

cut 1 and
1 reversed

12″ side — background

8″ handle

fold

12″ handle

8″ side — background

Colonial Basket

4, 8 and 12-inch sizes
Eight Patch, add seam allowance

Colonial basket is a good sitting-up on the block pattern for those projects that you cannot use a basket on the diagonal. The bottom half is pieced of triangles with a shaped handle appliqued on the top that is quite different from the traditional curved handles. The 8-inch size was used for pockets on the front of the vest pictured on the cover.

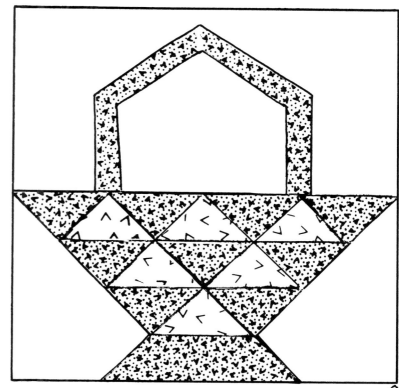

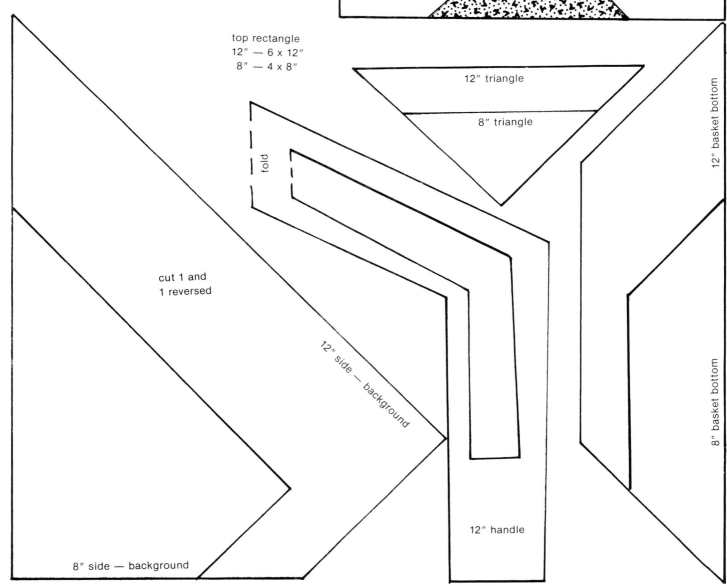

top rectangle
12" — 6 x 12"
8" — 4 x 8"

fold

12" triangle

8" triangle

12" basket bottom

cut 1 and
1 reversed

12" side — background

8" basket bottom

12" handle

8" side — background

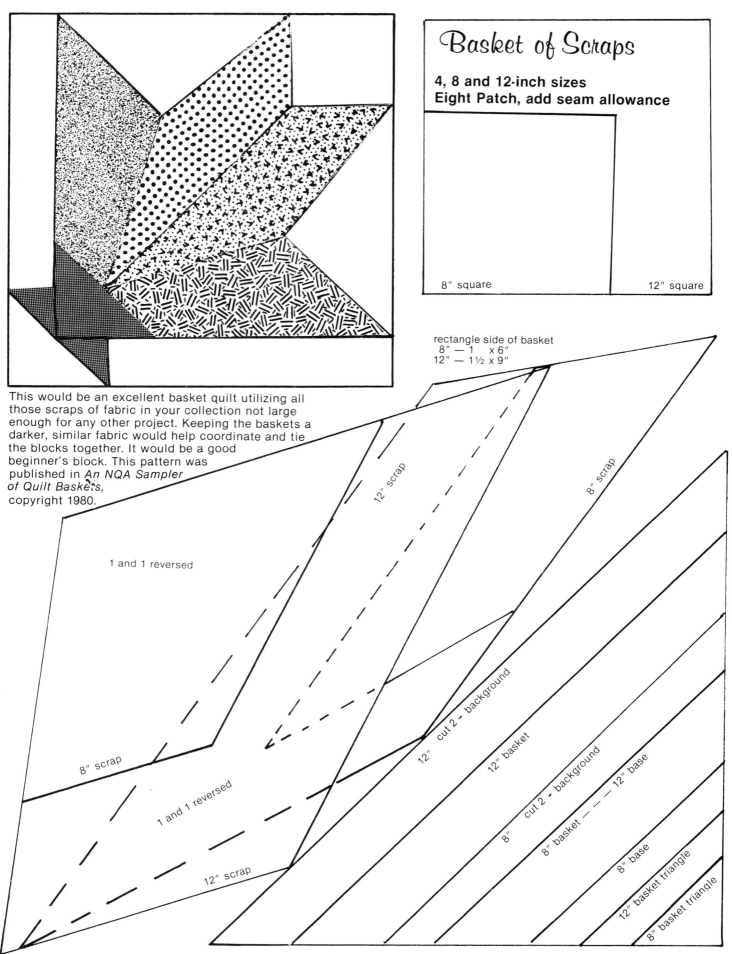

Basket of Scraps

4, 8 and 12-inch sizes
Eight Patch, add seam allowance

8" square

12" square

This would be an excellent basket quilt utilizing all those scraps of fabric in your collection not large enough for any other project. Keeping the baskets a darker, similar fabric would help coordinate and tie the blocks together. It would be a good beginner's block. This pattern was published in *An NQA Sampler of Quilt Baskets,* copyright 1980.

rectangle side of basket
8" — 1 x 6"
12" — 1½ x 9"

12" scrap

8" scrap

1 and 1 reversed

8" scrap

1 and 1 reversed

12" scrap

12" cut 2 - background

12" basket

8" cut 2 - background

12" basket

8" basket — — 12" base

8" base

12" basket triangle

8" basket triangle

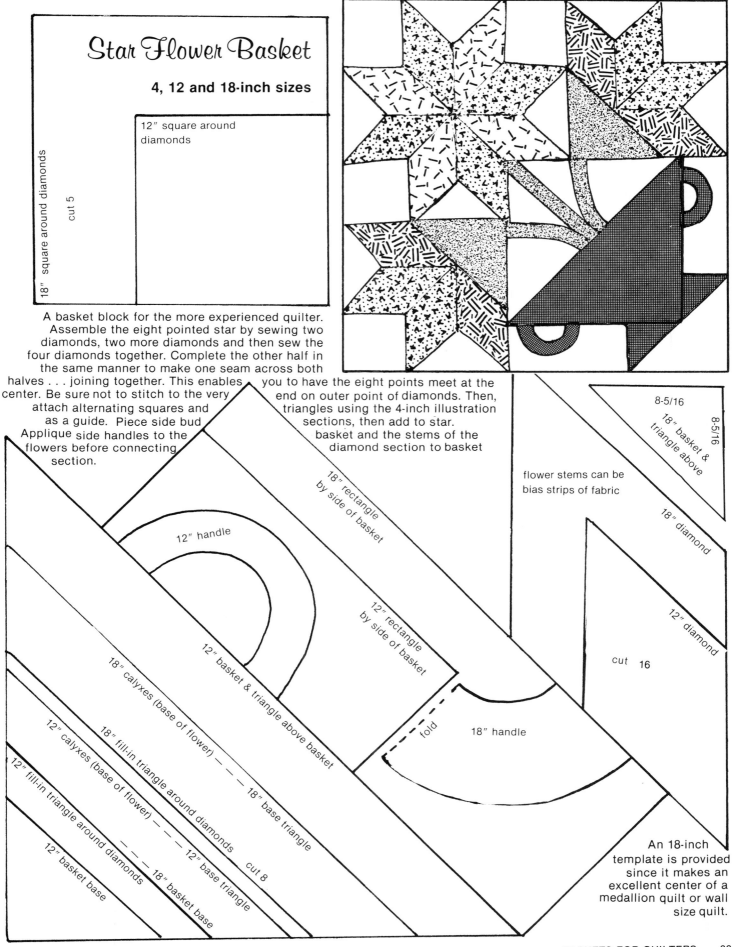

Star Flower Basket

4, 12 and 18-inch sizes

18" square around diamonds   cut 5

12" square around diamonds

A basket block for the more experienced quilter. Assemble the eight pointed star by sewing two diamonds, two more diamonds and then sew the four diamonds together. Complete the other half in the same manner to make one seam across both halves . . . joining together. This enables you to have the eight points meet at the center. Be sure not to stitch to the very end on outer point of diamonds. Then, attach alternating squares and triangles using the 4-inch illustration as a guide. Piece side bud sections, then add to star. Applique side handles to the basket and the stems of the flowers before connecting diamond section to basket section.

flower stems can be bias strips of fabric

12" handle

18" rectangle by side of basket

12" rectangle by side of basket

12" basket & triangle above basket

18" calyxes (base of flower) — — — 18" base triangle

18" fill-in triangle around diamonds   cut 8

12" calyxes (base of flower) — — — 12" base triangle

12" fill-in triangle around diamonds — — — 18" basket base

12" basket base

fold

18" handle

8-5/16
18" basket & triangle above
8-5/16

18" diamond

12" diamond

cut 16

An 18-inch template is provided since it makes an excellent center of a medallion quilt or wall size quilt.

Applique Baskets

A sampling of different basket shapes highlights the applique section. Care has been taken to eliminate some baskets because of the similarity to the baskets selected for inclusion.

There is also a feeling that a basket is not a basket unless it has a handle. A number of basket patterns without handles look more like a container for flowers rather than a basket. Subsequently, only patterns with handles are included in this book.

Baskets that are pieced and then appliqued to a block have also been eliminated . . . only completely appliqued patterns are illustrated.

All block templates are designed for a 12-inch block. This size is also easily adapted to a 14-inch or 15-inch block . . . providing a more airy feeling and more open space for quilting.

Additionally, a few tips are passed along to help change attitudes from "Oh no, it's an applique block!" to "What a beautiful block of applique."

Figuring Yardage

Figuring yardage for an applique quilt is easier than for a pieced quilt top. Just determine what size the applique background block is to be, how many of that size will fit across the width of your fabric, and multiply to obtain yardage requirements. For example, a 2½-yard length of yard goods will yield twenty-one 12½-inch x 12½-inch blocks (½-inch for seam allowance/¼-inch on each side). Completed block size is 12 inches by 12 inches.

You would be cutting out three blocks across the 44-inch to 45-inch fabric . . . seven times down. This will give you a quilt top four blocks across by five blocks down with an additional block for an accompanying pillow. Quilt top will be 48 inches by 60 inches before adding stripping and borders. For a twin bed applique quilt, see drawing on page 35.

Now for your first "tip." Before you start making your quilt top, put a pillow together. For one, it will give you practice with the pattern and for another, you will be able to visually see what the design looks like in your fabric choices. Once you have made the pillow, you will have a better idea of whether you will enjoy making a complete quilt of the pattern . . . both to applique and to quilt.

After deciding to proceed, cut out the required number of blocks from prewashed fabric . . . sealing all parts including background fabric for each block in individual plastic baggies. This solves two problems now and avoids other problems later on. First, you will know immediately that there is enough fabric to do the quilt. If you have ever made a quilt and run out of a particular print or solid at the 18th or 19th block, you already know the importance of this step.

Then, heaven forbid, should your granddaughter find this unfinished quilt in the attic, she will be able to complete the entire quilt since all parts and parcels are right there. Too often a student has come to class or a quilter will stop by with a few of Grandmother's or Aunt Martha's blocks that would make a beautiful quilt . . . only to discover not enough is there. It is very difficult to match solid fabrics within a year or two, yet alone many years down the road. And prints can be impossible.

When cutting out the background blocks, insert a pin to indicate the up and down grain of the fabric. Position all applique blocks for a particular project on the same grain line (up and down or across). It might not be apparent, but under certain lights, the cross grainline will have a different color tone than the up and down grainline.

In making a basket quilt, problems arise because many of the blocks are on the diagonal of the background block.

The lengthways straight grain of the fabric has to be planned with the blocks facing whichever way they are going to stand in the quilt. For example, in the mauve and blue applique quilt on the back cover, care was taken to make sure that the baskets were angled towards the center. To avoid the fabric looking like two different shadings of the background blocks, half were appliqued towards the center one way and half were appliqued towards the center the other way of the straight grain.

Now for a few "applique tips"! Review the assembly illustrations. Try one way, and if that does not work for you, try another, then another, until you find the one way that makes applique fun (if not fun, tolerable) and gives you the best possible, neatest applique piece of stitchery. This is not to say you cannot use different applique techniques in the same quilt. For some shapes you might applique one way, but a circle or unique shape might require another way to best applique the fabric shape onto the block.

Select a tightly woven 100 percent cotton fabric that will give you a clean cut edge. If it ravels at all, it will be very difficult to obtain a neatly finished applique block. You will be spending the same amount of time appliqueing whether you purchase quality fabric or fabric that will wear or fade quickly. The best quality fabric you can afford is the right fabric for your project.

For best results, regular thread is recommended. Also, use a color that best matches the individual piece you are appliqueing at the time. When using a marking pencil, pen or chalk, pretest them to be sure they are removable from your particular fabric. Always prewash all pieces of fabric to avoid shrinkage or color running. This precaution will save a flood of tears after putting hours of work into your project only to discover later that the fabric shrinks or colors run.

Add whatever seam allowance you prefer. Some people use the standard quilter's 1/4-inch, others prefer a little less, about 3/16-inch. If seam allowance is only 1/8-inch, it is just too little to hold properly. The advantage of 3/16-inch is that sometimes 1/4-inch is too bulky and presents problems going around circles and curves. Much as you would clip curves in sewing, clipping of curves in applique is essential. See illustration.

Next, trace around the template in this book and cut out a paper pattern. Glue this pattern to a firmer substance like quilter's transparent plastic, lightweight cardboard, or light sandpaper. Since seam allowances have not been included in the patterns, you will have to add them . . . either to the template or to your fabric.

Some quilters prefer to make the template the actual size flower, leaf or whatever shape is needed . . . trace around the template on the wrong side of the fabric . . . and add seam allowance as it is cut out. Other quilters like to lightly trace their template on the right side as this gives them a line they can readily see to turn under.

The problem with this second method is that if the shapes need to be changed ever so slightly to cover or connect to another piece, the drawn line is on the outside of the work instead of turned under. If it is a stubborn fabric to turn under, or a tricky shape, or to be exact, you may press the fabric over a lightweight cardboard or sandpaper template (no plastic please). Another way is to baste the seam allowance under before basting the piece to the background block. Or, you may turn under the seam allowance as you go along appliqueing it down.

Prepare the background block before basting on your pieces. The block should be prewashed and on the straight grain of the fabric.

Fold in half diagonally both ways, and in half crossways and lengthways. Finger press or if that does not show, lightly press with an iron. This will assure baskets that will stand straight . . . either on the diagonal of the block (if that is their design) or on the straight up and down.

Baste all applique pieces in place, allowing for seam allowances and overlapping where required. Blind stitch in place . . . just coming through the folded-under seam allowance so that your stitches do not show. This is the reason the color of thread should match the piece being appliqued, as it helps to blend in even more if the thread should show a little. Start with the underneath pieces of the design first and then work out to the overlapping pieces.

Following pages have fourteen applique block designs for a standard 12-inch block. How they are designed to sit on a block is illustrated on each page. The center basket medallion is made up of a basket oval of the simple basket pattern and the center basket is strips of fabric appliqued down to give the basket shape.

To duplicate, these strips should be cut 1 inch wide. This provides a 1/4-inch seam allowance on each side with final size of each strip being 1/2 inch. Cut strips on the bias of the fabric unless, as in the case of the quilt pictured, you may wish to take advantage of stripe fabric. Curve shaped baskets would have to be of bias fabric.

Or, as an alternate, you may take any of the basket shapes you like, putting your own flower choices in the block. Your knowledge of the color, size and shapes of the different flowers and traditional flower arrangement guidelines will help you create your very own basket quilt or quilt block.

This is the main reason why so many different options are presented in this book . . . do your own thing . . . create a quilt that is uniquely yours . . . for there is no better feeling than designing your very own quilt or quilt block.

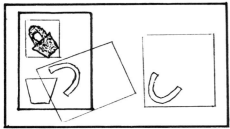
Trace pattern and make template accurately.

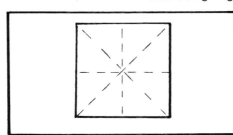
Square off block for placement.

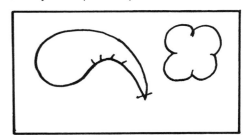
Clip points and curves.

Press over template for accuracy; or baste edges under; or turn under seam as you stitch to block.

Baste on block for placement.

Blind stitch applique in place.

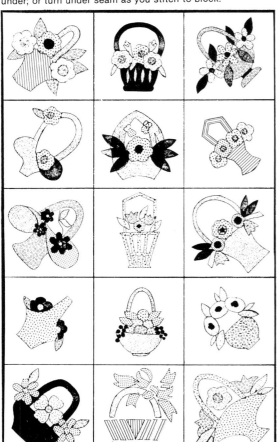

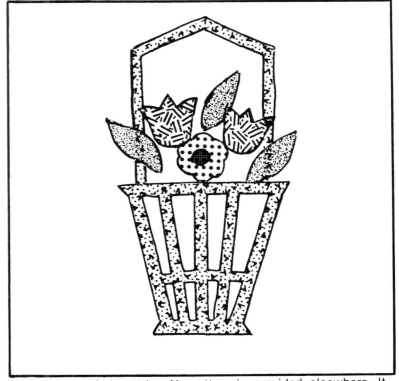
Basket made of bias strips. No pattern is provided elsewhere. It is provided here as a setting possibility for the bias strip basket. Use various leaves and flowers from the following pages to fill your basket.

Floral Handle Basket

4 and 12-inch sizes
14 Pieces, add seam allowance

This pattern was pictured in a 1979 *Quilt World* article, "Garden of Quilt Blocks." Although it was not named in that article, the title "Basket with Floral Handle" is provided here for identification purposes. The flowers themselves form a handle illusion.

This simple basket and handle (all of a single piece of fabric) was drawn by the author to use in the center medallion section of the applique quilt pictured on the back cover. It was carried out to the four corners to anchor the vine border.

fold

Fancy Bow Basket

4 and 12-inch sizes
20 Pieces, add seam allowance

Published in *Family Circle,* February, 1980. This basket was originally done in reverse applique. Since the other baskets in the quilt pictured on the back cover were appliqued, applique was chosen over reverse applique. *Family Circle* offered this in pillow or quilt kit form. What a delightful addition to the basket designs that are planned to sit on the square of the fabric!

cut 3 and 3 reversed

Kathy's Basket

4 and 12-inch sizes
15 Pieces, add seam allowance

A friend brought over a basket of her own design done out of leather. It gives a good opportunity to try some reverse applique in the slits in the basket. Cut a piece of fabric that is just a little smaller than the actual basket, then pin in place. After appliqueing down the basket outside edges, carefully cut the four slits, turn under edges so that the second underneath fabric shows through the four openings. This pattern sits on the square of the block.

fold

Fruit Basket

**4 and 12-inch sizes
12 Pieces (plus grapes),
add seam allowance**

Published in *Needlecraft,* June 1929. Since a
Garden Club friend did not approve of the blue and
lavender flowers used in the applique sampler on
the back cover, she searched for a basket using the
right colors. This fruit basket block could have pink
peaches, purple plums, burgundy apples and blue
grapes for a more realistic effect.

fold

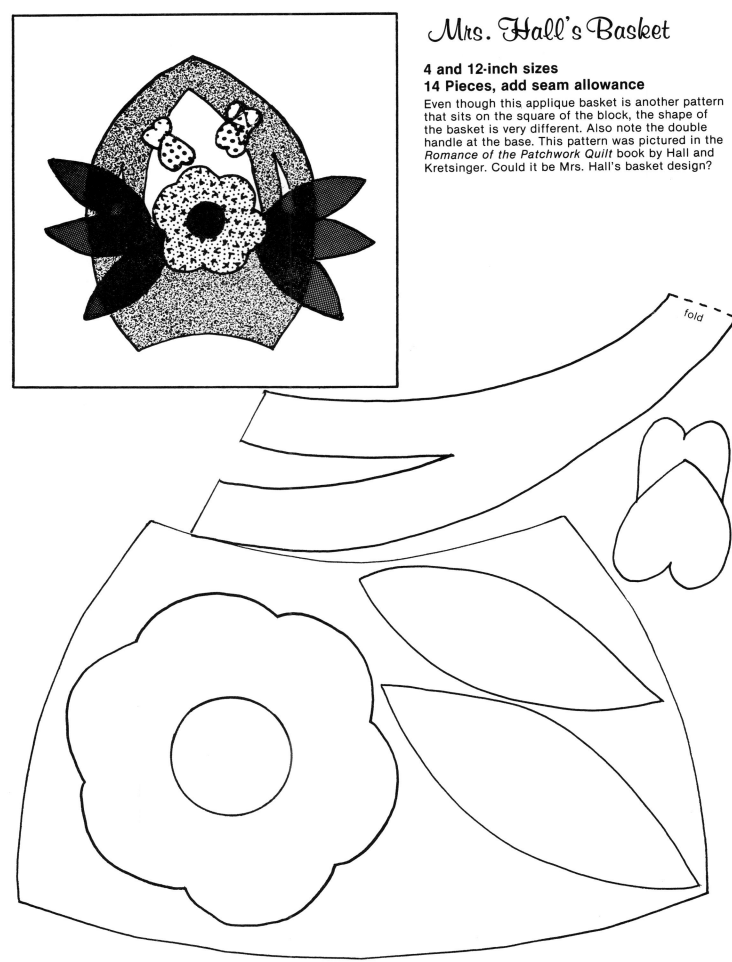

Mrs. Hall's Basket

4 and 12-inch sizes
14 Pieces, add seam allowance

Even though this applique basket is another pattern that sits on the square of the block, the shape of the basket is very different. Also note the double handle at the base. This pattern was pictured in the *Romance of the Patchwork Quilt* book by Hall and Kretsinger. Could it be Mrs. Hall's basket design?

fold

fold

Daisy Basket

4 and 12-inch sizes
27 Pieces, add seam allowance

This three-piece basket with the overhanging sides makes a beautiful block done individually or in a larger size. Match A to A and B to B for basket placement on the block. To help emphasize the overhanging separate pieces, cut a bias piece of darker or lighter coordinating fabric, then insert as you are appliqueing the overlapping part with approximately 1/8-inch showing. Or, you may choose to follow the 4-inch design of three separate coordinating pieces of fabric to achieve a three dimensional effect.

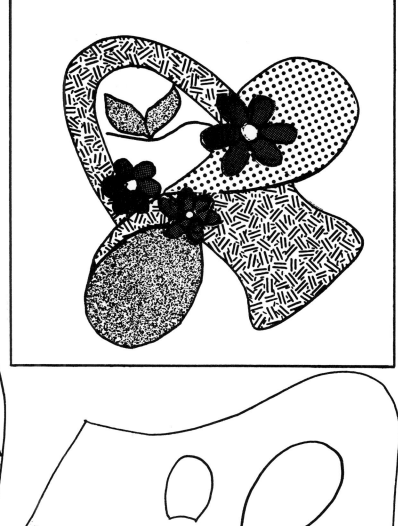

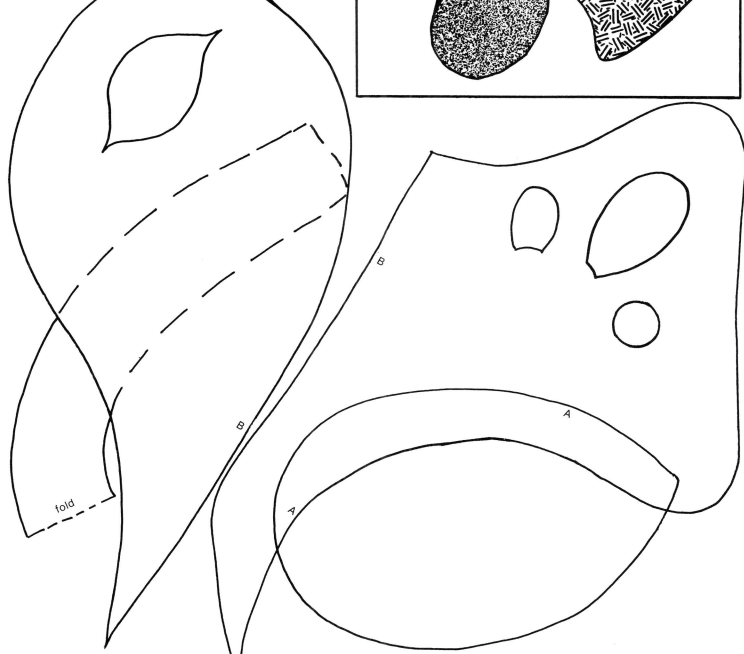

fold

B

B

A

A

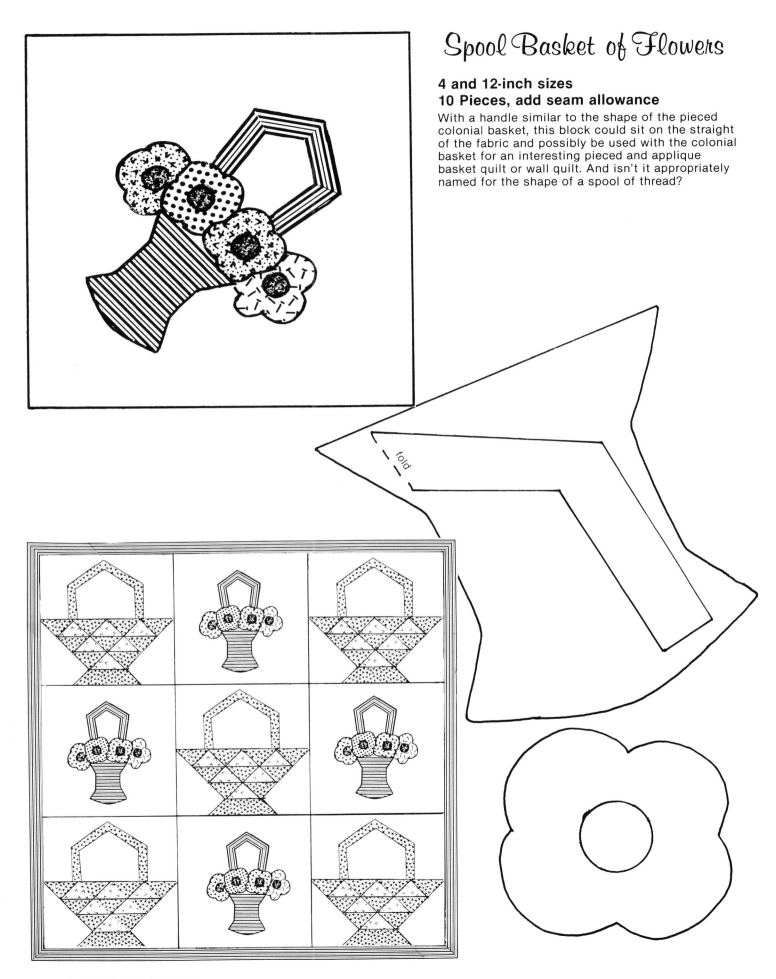

Spool Basket of Flowers

4 and 12-inch sizes
10 Pieces, add seam allowance

With a handle similar to the shape of the pieced colonial basket, this block could sit on the straight of the fabric and possibly be used with the colonial basket for an interesting pieced and applique basket quilt or wall quilt. And isn't it appropriately named for the shape of a spool of thread?

fold

Patch Basket

4 and 12-inch sizes
25 Pieces, add seam allowance

A *Grandma Dexter* pattern from the 1930's, Dexter Yarn and Thread Co. This is similar to the daisy basket in its floral arrangement, but offers a pleasant variation in the shape of the basket.

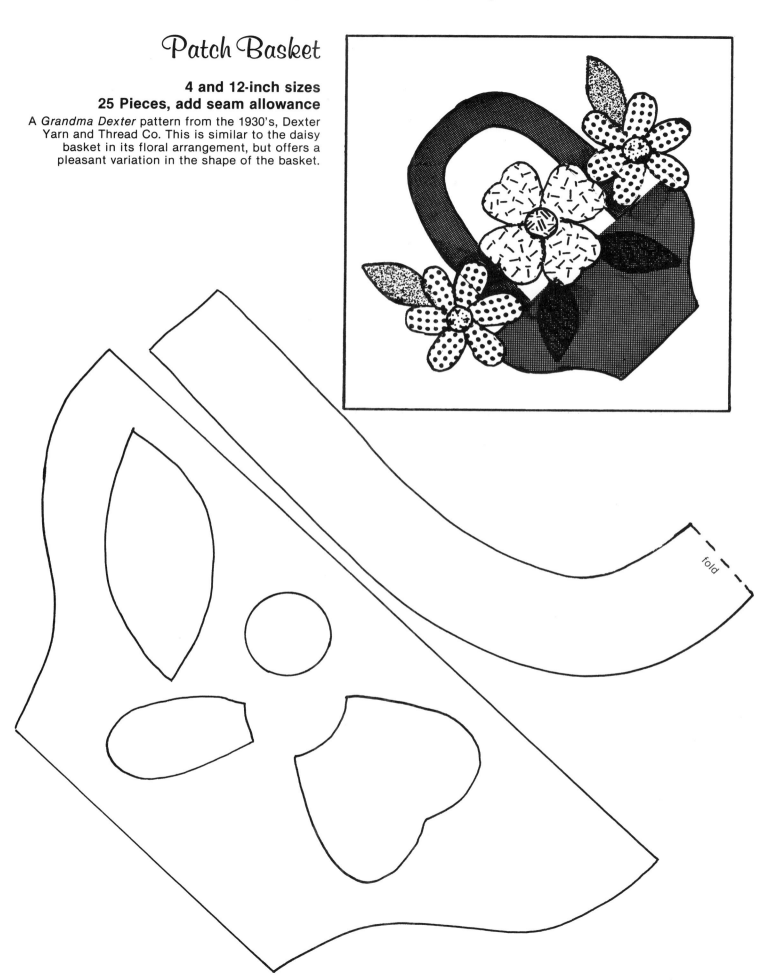

fold

Maude Hare's Basket

4 and 12-inch sizes
19 Pieces, add seam allowance

Maude Hare's Basket generates a feeling of springtime with its floral shapes . . . and don't you just love the name? The tulip shape flower that drops down over the side can be one piece or you can do a little shading with a lighter or darker tip.

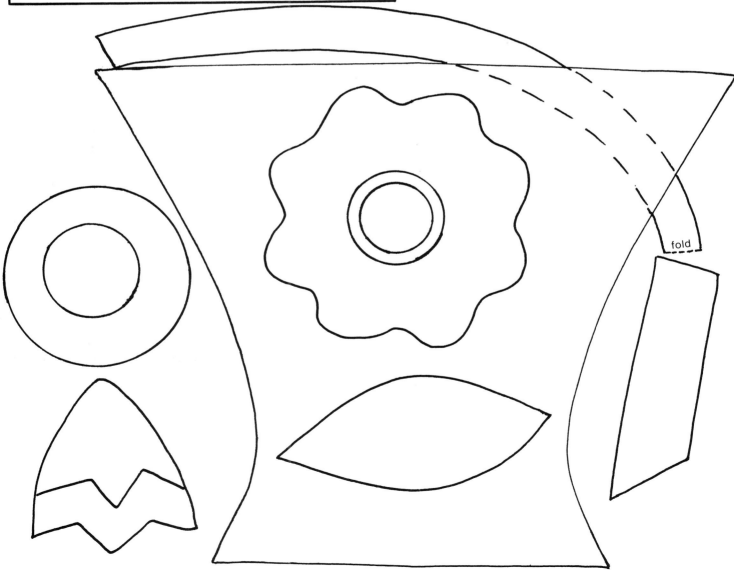

fold

Basket Patch

4 and 12-inch sizes
13 Pieces, add seam allowance

Although this basket is similar in shape to a couple other baskets, the handle is fully visible on one side and halfway down on the other side because of the flower arrangement.

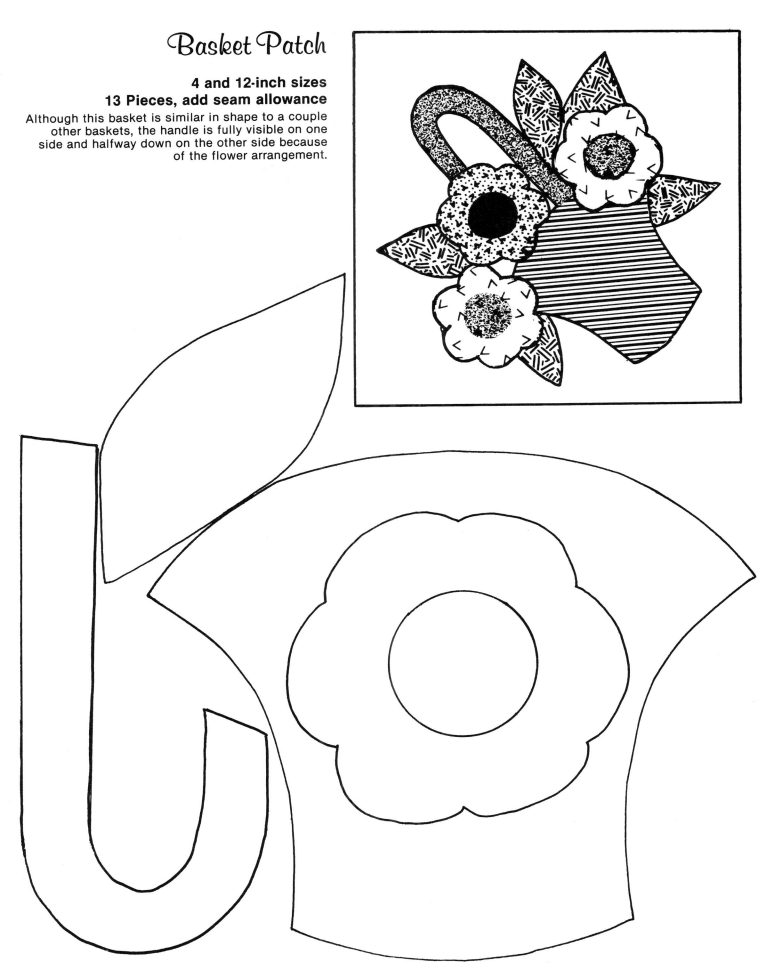

Small Basket
with Flowers

4 and 12-inch sizes
9 Pieces, add seam allowance

Published in the *Quilt World Omnibook*, Spring 1980. This delicate, airy basket provides ample room for quilting. It is probably the easiest of the applique blocks chosen for this book and would be an excellent block to begin with.

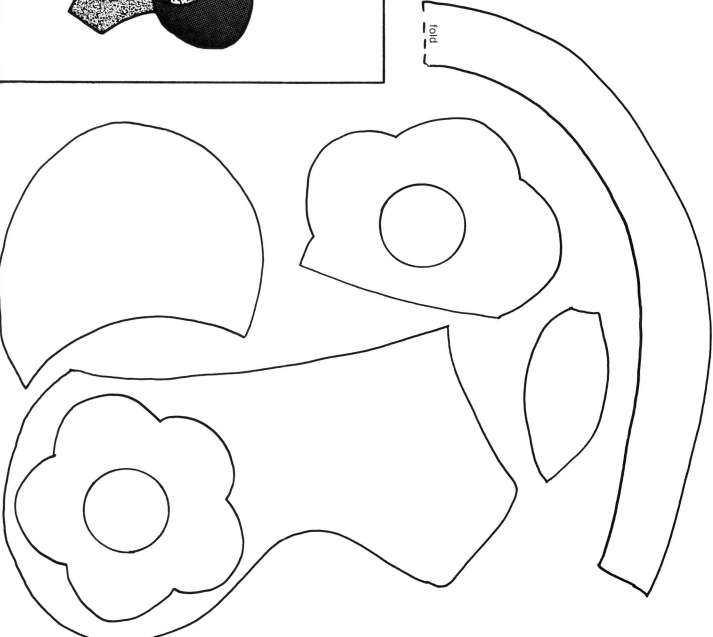

fold

May Basket

4 and 12-inch sizes
10 Pieces, add seam allowance

This is possibly the most common of all of the applique baskets. It is a well-balanced diagonal block stretching to all four corners.

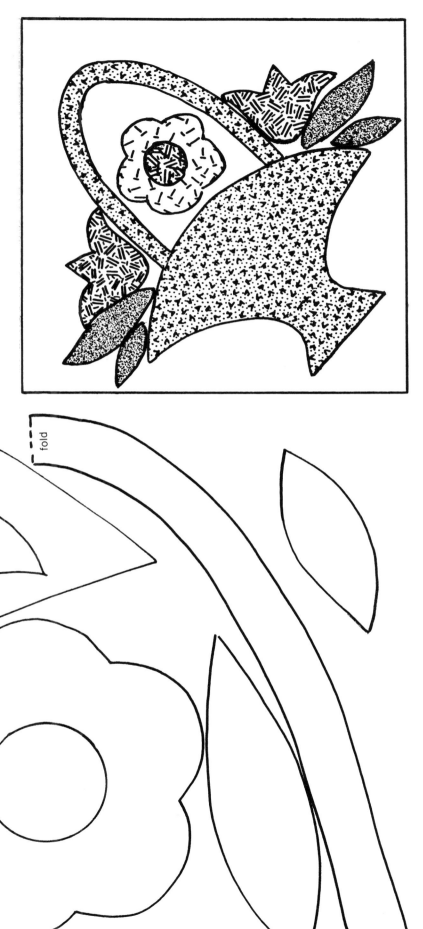

fold

fold

Side View Basket

4 and 12-inch sizes
7 Pieces, add seam allowance

A pattern first published in 1935 edition of the *Kansas City Star.* It features a very different handle treatment from all the other baskets. Although the newspaper article just called it a basket, "Side View Basket" description provides a readily recognizable identification. This pattern rates right up there with the small basket with flowers as a beginning applique block.

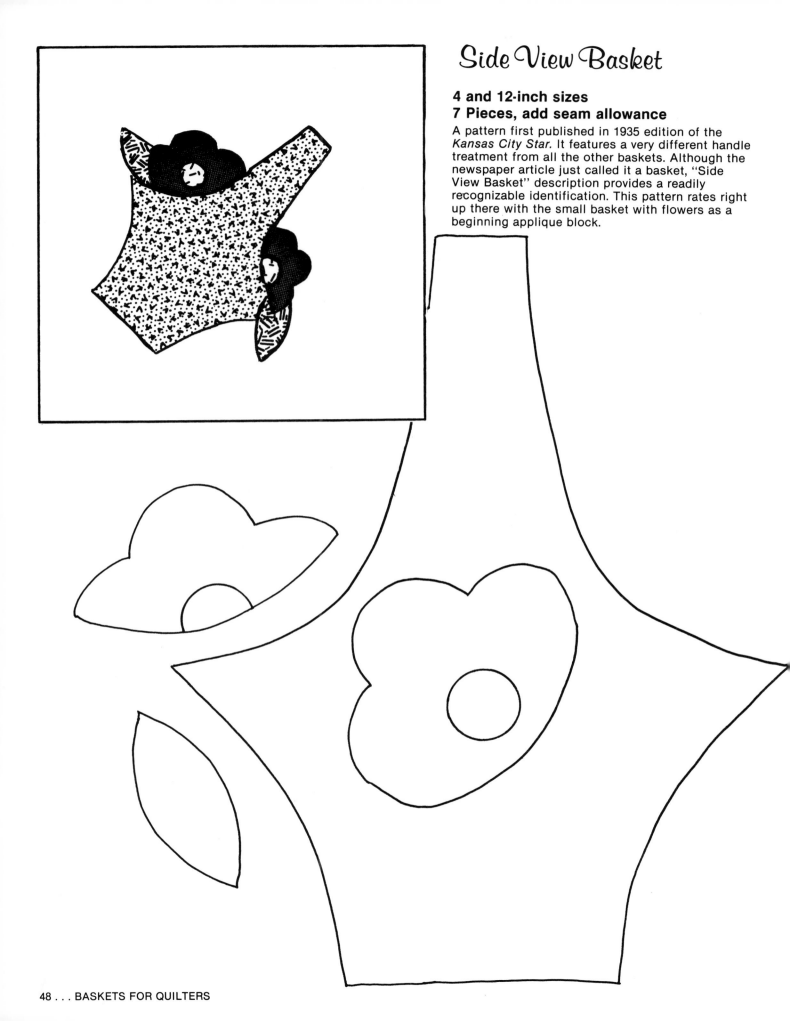

Basket of Daisies

4 and 12-inch sizes
28 Pieces, add seam allowance

If the handle were left off, this basket would look more like a pedestal vase. The daisies are similar to the daisy basket shape but pattern incorporates a totally different pedestal basket shape.

fold

Wearable Baskets

Basket patterns are ideally suited for incorporating into various articles of clothing. The 8-inch baskets throughout this book would be excellent for the larger back area of a vest or jacket. For this type of garment, baskets set on the diagonal of the block are preferred since the 8-inch block measures 11-1/4 inches across kitty-corner to kitty-corner. Fill in around the block and build down to the bottom of the garment with the string method of quilting. An example is shown on the cover.

The 8-inch size that sets square on the block also works well for the bottom front of a vest or jacket. An ideal way to use baskets on the front of a garment is as a visual anchor for a floral design going up and down the front.

Bottom front garment baskets may also have a utilitarian function as a pocket. Instructions for making pockets are on page 14 in the "pieced" section of this book.

Another good basket pattern for clothing is a 10-inch by 12-inch size rectangle basket as it is already the shape to provide a more slimming line. Up and down lines in clothing are much more flattering to most figures than lines going across.

The white-on-white, just quilted jacket on the back cover utilizes a basket as the basic design on the back of the jacket with a bouquet of flowers circling the entire jacket. To duplicate, draw on the design, then baste very carefully the three layers (top, batting and backing or lining), quilt, bind off all edges, and add any finishing touches you feel are necessary. You now have an exquisite evening jacket ready to wear. It is recommended that you sew the side seams together and leave the shoulder seams to sew after the garment is quilted and finished (see illustration). After all quilting is completed, sew the shoulder seams on the outside with your sewing machine, then slipstitch the batting together and finish by sewing the lining seam by hand. The basket pattern used for the jacket pictured was the 12-inch size orange basket.

Another excellent spot to wear a basket is on the bib of an apron. Once again, the 8-inch standing upright basket pattern is recommended since it will make up nicely into a pocket. For apron skirt pockets, a pleasant variation would be to use the diagonal 8-inch basket. Three functional baskets in one apron will be a special, uniquely yours, gift for a friend or member of the family.

In all of the clothing garments presented here, standard commercially available patterns were used as the basic pattern. A word of caution . . . quilted clothing works best on patterns without any darts or patterns that have a straighter line.

On your next wearable, blend in some basket patterns or basket pockets to transform the garment into a delightful prize.

Baskets in Clothing